DEPRESSION

Also by Elaine Fantle Shimberg

STROKES: What Families Should Know
RELIEF FROM IBS   Irritable Bowel Syndrome

DEPRESSION

What Families Should Know

Elaine Fantle Shimberg

BALLANTINE BOOKS • NEW YORK

Copyright © 1991 by Elaine Fantle Shimberg

All rights reserved under International and Pan-American Copyright Conventions. Published in the United States by Ballantine Books, a division of Random House, Inc., New York, and simultaneously in Canada by Random House of Canada Limited, Toronto.

http://www.randomhouse.com

Library of Congress Catalog Card Number: 96-96616

ISBN: 345-41023-8

Manufactured in the United States of America

First Mass Market Edition: January 1992
First Trade Edition: August 1996

10 9 8 7 6 5 4 3 2 1

To My Children

Andy, Betsy, Kasey, Michael, and Scott
who kept me laughing

Table of Contents

Author's Note

The information contained in this book reflects the author's experience, interviews, and research and is in no way intended to replace professional medical advice. Specific medical and psychological opinions can only be given by a qualified physician or therapist who knows the depressed patient, his or her particular medical and psychological history, and other relevant data. Always consult a health care professional.

Acknowledgments

My deepest appreciation to Gerald L. Klerman, M.D.; Ellen Frank, Ph.D.; and Sol Gordon, Ph.D. for their valuable time and assistance. Thanks also to Joseph Lupo, M.D.; Robert Schaffer, Ph.D.; Donald A. Williamson, Ph.D.; Madelaine M. Wohlreich, M.D.; Rudolf H. Moos, Ph.D.; Anne S. Lockey, M.D.; and Eric Pfeiffer, M.D. A most special thanks to my editor, Cheryl D. Woodruff, for her personal encouragement and to my agents Herb and Nancy Katz, who believed in this project from the very beginning and helped to keep me from becoming depressed while writing it.

The anecdotes used in this book are based on factual material gathered through interviews—both formal and informal—with over one hundred men, women, and young people who were willing to share their experiences of living with a loved one's depression. As so many of them requested anonymity, I have chosen to protect their privacy by blending identities and altering ages, names, professions, and other characteristics. In some cases the anecdote used is actually a blending of two or more actual cases. I thank all these "experts," who by sharing their thoughts with me allowed me the opportunity to share them with many others, perpetuating what Dr. Sol Gordon calls his "each one reach one" philosophy.

=== 1 ===

The Dynamics of Depression

"I'm so exhausted," my friend of many years told me in a slow, maddening monotone, as she toyed with the salad on her plate. "Everything's just too much effort. It's like a veil's settled over my face, and I can't see beyond it." Tears rolled down her cheeks.

"It's not just me," she continued. "Everything's falling apart. Paul seems distant and preoccupied. He and the kids keep nagging at me to 'pull myself together . . . get involved in volunteer work.' They don't seem to understand that most days I can't even get myself out of bed, let alone get dressed. What's happening to me? What's happened to our family? We used to be so happy. Everything used to be perfect."

I looked silently at my friend, Babs, wishing that this painful lunch (which I had insisted upon) would soon be over. Although I ached at her sadness, I was keenly aware that I also felt frustrated and, yes, even angry at her for being this way. Why couldn't she be the way she used to be?

"The kids seem out of hand like everything else," she sighed. "Diane's too thin. She just won't eat anything. Marcy's gotten in with a bad crowd. Even Paul acts like he can't wait to get out of the house . . . away from me." She droned on. "We used to be so close. All of us. . . ."

Her flat tone made my mind wander. Tuning her out,

1

I glanced outside the restaurant at the bleak scene—bare branches etched against the soot-covered snow. I shivered, not from cold, but rather from the hopelessness I heard in Babs's voice. Unconsciously I drew away, as though to protect myself from ''catching'' her malaise.

What had happened to my friend? What was eroding her family's former cohesiveness? My husband and I had known Babs and Paul since college days, their children since birth. This family, at least to outsiders, appeared to be the stuff of Norman Rockwell paintings. We had been in their home many times. It usually had been filled with laughter, music, books, and stimulating conversation.

But something changed as the children grew older. We noted subtle signs, but, involved in our own busy lives, we were slow to identify the problem. We hadn't noticed our gradual distancing ourselves from these friends; it was just something that happened.

They stopped giving the dinner parties they had been famous for; their friends (including us) stopped including them at social functions: they cancelled out too often and at the last minute. Either Paul was ''working late'' or Babs was ''ill.'' We, who had considered ourselves good friends, stopped thinking to call Babs and Paul when we decided, spur of the moment, to go out to dinner or to a movie. Without analyzing why, we had withdrawn because . . . because, now that we compared notes, they just weren't fun to be with anymore.

But it was more than that. We discovered that we both actually felt dispirited and blue—actually uncomfortable—after being with them. Babs was always so tired, so sad, so negative. I often felt angry and depressed after just being on the phone with her.

It was then we realized, with a start, that Babs was suffering from depression. What was worse, Paul and their children had become ''shadow patients'' and were affected as well. Even we, their friends, were not immune. We all had been tainted with the effects of Babs's depression; we all were suffering from the fallout of depression.

As a medical writer, it bothered me that I should have been so unaware of Babs's depression and its effects on her family and friends. As both writer and friend, I was surprised at the duplicity practiced by all of us as we tried to pretend that nothing had changed. "Babs was tired." "Babs had flu." Nothing was wrong; everything was wonderful. The myth of their happy and well-functioning family must be preserved at all costs, and we, their friends, were accomplices in this farce.

What's more, as we all became immersed in our roles, there was some question that anyone really wanted Babs to recover; that is, to change—to become, in effect, a different person. Of course, none of us would have ever admitted that nor, probably, ever actually realized it. Even depressed, the old Babs, the familiar Babs, was somehow easier to have around than a "new" Babs might be. We took comfort in the familiar. Things "worked" before, at least for us. The fact that the same system, which functioned so smoothly for us and filled *our* needs, might be poisoning her and triggering her depression wasn't even whispered.

For Babs to recover from her depression meant that she probably would have to make changes in her life. But those changes were bound to have a ripple effect, affecting Babs, her family, and even her friends. We also might have to change in order to help her. Were we willing to? Rather than answer, we skirted the issue. It was easier to bemoan her depressed state, to feel sorry for the way she had become, and to perpetuate the status quo, than to support her struggle to make those changes that would permit her to overcome her depression.

Had Babs been afflicted by almost any other type of serious illness—a heart attack, cancer, diabetes, or stroke—we might have been more sympathetic, more supportive. But she was "only" depressed. She didn't even look sick, only sad. The silent message we all shared

was that if she would just "get her act together," she'd
be fine.

Depression is a family problem

These dilemmas were the stimuli for this book, *Depression: What Families Should Know*. For far too many
years depression has been kept hidden in the closet. By
unspoken agreement, no one in the family mentioned the
"D" word. But that didn't make it go away. Denying its
existence didn't make the depressed person feel any better, and it certainly didn't help the family learn to cope
with depression's side effects.

It's time to face the foe, first by acknowledging its
existence, then by understanding what it is and what it
does to those it attacks. Only when armed with this
knowledge can a family circle the wagons around its depressed member and become fully supportive. It's vital
for us to understand depression because, like it or not,
we become involved in a family member's depression.
We feed into it, affecting it (both positively and nega-
tively) in various ways. At the same time we are considerably affected by it. Depression is like a giant wheel
that rolls back and forth endlessly for family members
and the depressed alike until someone or something
comes along to help apply the brakes.

We, as a family, *can* help to apply those brakes and
help a loved one suffering from depression, but we must
understand its dynamics and, at the same time, protect
ourselves from its grasp.

There is, unfortunately, no one answer that fits everyone. Just as each of us is different, even from our brother
or sister, each family unit is unique, and each individual
in a particular family may react differently to the depressed person. Our reaction depends upon many different factors, including our own emotional makeup, and
what the illness represents to us personally (Is it a power
struggle, fear of the loss of love and support from the

person who is ill, concern over financial affairs, or humiliation that others may know of a loved one's depression?). Our reaction may vary as well according to what else is going on in our life at that particular time, such as business or personal problems, ill health, and so on.

Nevertheless, it often helps to know that others have lived with and through the overwhelming emotions that wash down upon you when someone you care about is depressed. I have interviewed, both formally and informally, over one hundred people who have struggled to cope with the problems that arise when a close family member or friend suffers from depression. Suggestions from these fellow travelers, along with specific information from psychologists, psychiatrists, pediatricians, neurologists, teachers, clergy, and other professionals who deal with depression are also included in this book.

Family can be part of the solution

I am a medical writer, not a physician. Although I have studied psychology, I am not a psychologist or psychiatrist. As a lay person, I have cursed my ignorance of the mechanics of depression, wondered about the myths that surround it, and accepted guilt that wasn't mine because someone I cared for was depressed and I didn't know what to do.

This book is for others who want to help a loved one but feel helpless. Unlike many other books on depression, it is not filled with medical jargon that may be confusing to a lay person or endless research data that seems to have little bearing on what's actually going on in your day-to-day life. It is not written for the theorist, in the abstract, but for families who want information they can use NOW. The professionals who have shared their expertise with me have allowed me to paraphrase their thoughts in lay language.

"Make this a working book," said one psychologist who not only granted an interview but also agreed to read over the final manuscript. "If it doesn't work for the reader, it can't help them work with someone who's depressed."

Depression is "an infectious disorder"

Most of us will need the information in this book sometime in our lives. Depression is hardly a rare disorder. It's estimated that one out of every ten of us will suffer from serious depression at some point in our lives. Children as well as adults—even infants as young as three months—may suffer from depression.

Women seem to be twice as likely as men to suffer from depression. Experts offer numerous theories for this, ranging from genetic to hormonal or social. Author Harriet Goldhor Lerner, Ph.D., of the Menninger Clinic suggests that ". . . women frequently sacrifice the 'I' in the service of 'togetherness' thus assuming a de-selfed position in relationships."[1] Another study suggests that women become depressed more easily than men because they become more concerned about other people's problems and are more sensitive to their needs.[2] Still others suggest that the reasons are probably as varied as the women themselves and their particular situations. For our purposes, however, it is probably less important to know *why* women become more easily depressed than men and more vital to learn what we can do to help those specific women in our lives who are depressed.

Experts figure that in any given year about 4 percent of the population of the United States suffers from major depression. Depression, however, does not happen in a vacuum. When one family member is depressed, it often spreads throughout the rest of the family like a creeping but steady lava flow. That's why depression is often considered to be "an infectious disorder."

One "thirtysomething" woman likened depression in her family to one of those creatures in a monster movie. "You know it's out there," she said, "and that it's alive.

You even know which shadow it's hiding in. But just when you think you've found a safe hiding spot, it oozes in under the door and grabs you."

She continued. "I can be feeling great, upbeat, and positive, then my mother, who's been depressed as long as I can remember, will call. I'll get a funny feeling in my stomach, feel my whole body stiffening, and have a sense of a tightening in my throat. It's hard to explain. It's almost as though I'm being enveloped by the depression monster. By the time I hang up, my sense of joy is gone, and it's almost impossible to recapture. I feel depressed and, even worse, know that I'm spreading the depression I've caught to my kids. It isn't just me that feels it either. If my husband happens to answer the phone first, *he* gets depressed. And she isn't even his mother!"

Others who have spouses or children who are depressed repeat similar stories.

"I traveled on the road for many years and made a good living for my wife and our kids," Abe said. "Everything seemed fine until the kids went away to college. Evelyn stopped teaching, even though she had always loved it. She said it made her too tired. She withdrew from everything she had been interested in before. I knew she was depressed and tried everything I could to help her. I quit the road and took one of the office positions. I did the cooking, the cleaning, and tried to make plans to do social things, but she just wasn't interested. Nothing I did seemed to help. At times I found myself feeling so depressed I could weep."

Another spouse, a forty-five-year-old insurance salesman, confided, "I've become a workaholic. My only pleasures come from my job and the people I meet through it. Most nights I stop somewhere to eat before coming home. I find it almost impossible to stay in good spirits when I do get home and see my wife. She looks so sad; everything she says is negative; she moves in slow motion. It makes me want to scream, so instead I just stay away. What's really scary is that when I stay home too much, like on the weekends, *I* start acting just like her.''

That's not surprising. Some experts estimate that people living with someone who is depressed have an 80 percent chance of becoming depressed themselves. But it works both ways. The family's reaction to the depressed member also affects him or her as well. The more you pull away in self-defense, the more the person feels rejected and isolated, and the depression may deepen. In some cases, according to Jim Orford, Senior Lecturer in Clinical Psychology at the University of Exeter, Great Britain, ''. . . the disorder (depression) may itself be part of the family's way of accommodating to preexisting tensions.''[3]

That doesn't mean that a family purposely goes out of its way to make one of its members depressed. It suggests instead that the family's coping mechanisms may be faulty and that its problems may tend to be handled in a dysfunctional way. Sadly the friction that often occurs within a family during someone's depression may remain among some of the members even after the depression goes away. It's unlikely that these family members were ever able to talk much about the depression when it was full-blown. Therefore, it's also probable that some relatives will continue to suffer from poor communication even after the worst is over.

Perhaps this book can ease some of the problems by bringing them out into the open. Often, seeing some of your thoughts or troubles spelled out on paper helps make them easier to face, to discuss, and to handle. The aim of this book is to:

- Let families know what depression is so that the members can recognize it and understand how it affects the functioning of the family system.
- Suggest techniques for family members to master in order to protect themselves from ''catching'' their loved one's depression.

- Offer ways in which the family can give support to its depressed member.

Depression: What Families Should Know deals with the many causes of depression and describes how depression reveals itself. It shows you how to determine when a loved one is just "down" and when he or she is struggling with a depression that requires professional treatment. Anecdotes shared by other family members facing this problem may help you to understand and accept that your feelings of anger, resentment, frustration, guilt, and fear are far from strange, "bad," or abnormal.

As depression is so very contagious, you'll also learn specific suggestions on how to protect yourself from absorbing someone's depression as well as how to improve your own coping mechanisms, strengthen communication skills, and minimize stress throughout most trying circumstances.

Serious depression always requires professional help and often medical treatment. This book describes various forms of modern treatment for depression along with their advantages and disadvantages. You'll also read suggestions on specific ways you can work with your depressed family member, explaining what you can realistically hope to achieve. It demonstrates ways to become aware of what's happening, how to encourage treatment, and where to find help. It also describes how to let someone know you care about him or her even though you're feeling frightened and frustrated.

You'll read about depression in children and the truth about suicide, learning what to do when you think someone is suicidal.

Don't figure that you can give this book to someone who's depressed and that he or she will then quickly snap out of the depression. It's unlikely that he or she would do more than glance through it. People who are seriously depressed usually feel too passive and exhausted to do anything requiring as much effort as reading. It just seems too strenuous and overwhelming. Chances are that the person also might deny being depressed and would feel there was no sense in reading about it. Even if he or she *would* admit to being depressed, most sufferers from depression feel that things are just too hopeless to change and that they are incapable of being helped. They are filled with despair and a sense of futility. This very passiveness can make family members both mystified and mad.

"Why won't she try to help herself?" the most understanding relative may shout in frustration. "She just sits there." But if she could do something, she would. Depression just kills the spirit. Yet it's probable that your loved one senses your frustration and feels badly about it, even though she is unable to change her behavior.

So although you can read the book and discuss parts of it with someone who is depressed, this book is really for you and for all family members (and friends) who are struggling through the quicksand of depression. I hope it helps keep you from being totally trapped. There *is* a way out for families struggling with depression, but, as with quicksand, you must be careful that, while attempting a rescue, you don't get pulled in, too.

Endnotes

1. Harriet Goldhor Lerner, Ph.D., "Female Depression: Self-Sacrifice and Self-Betrayal in Relationships," in *Women and Depression, A Lifespan Perspective*, ed. Ruth Formanek, Ph.D., and Anita Gurian, Ph.D., (New York: Springer Publishing Company, 1987), p.200.
2. R. Jay Turner and William R. Avison, "Gender and depression: assessing exposure and vulnerability to life events in a chronically strained population," *Journal of Nervous and Mental Disease*, 177 (August 1989):443-455.
3. Jim Orford, *Treating the Disorder, Treating the Family*, (Baltimore: The Johns Hopkins University Press, 1987), p.4.

2

Who Gets Depressed and Why?

Depression is an equal-opportunity disease. It affects both the rich and poor; educated and illiterate; black and white; male and female; Jew, Gentile, and atheist. It has no respect for age, afflicting both young and old alike.

Almost nobody escapes from depression; they either personally suffer from it or try to cope with a family member who is afflicted. It is the most common biological disorder seen in psychiatry today. You've probably been depressed at some point in your life. I have too. But we're hardly unique. Many famous people have suffered from bouts of depression.

Sir Winston Churchill struggled with depression for most of his adult life, calling it "the black dog." Authors Ernest Hemingway, William Styron, and Sylvia Plath, actress Patty Duke, and composers A. Claude Debussy and George Frideric Handel are just a few of depression's artistic victims. Rulers from King Saul to Queen Elizabeth I to Abraham Lincoln and, in modern times, former U.S. Senator Thomas Eagleton and Florida Governor Lawton Chiles have suffered from depression as have wives of politicians including first ladies Betty Ford and Barbara Bush. Former astronaut Buzz Aldrin fought against depression, and scores of movie and theatre stars

11

now openly admit doing battle with it. So you see, you
don't need to feel embarrassed if someone in your family
is suffering from depression right now. Unfortunately,
they're in good company.

Depression may be hard to detect

Although, according to a number of studies, one in
every five patients in a doctor's office is seriously depressed, it nevertheless remains misdiagnosed in 30 to
50 percent of patients. While some doctors fail to detect
depression because of poor diagnostic techniques and inadequate listening skills, depression often is masked—
consciously or otherwise—by the patient. He or she may
complain of headaches or other aches and pains, nausea
or faintness, or request sleeping pills for insomnia or
vitamins to correct fatigue, yet firmly deny feeling depressed.

For many people, admitting to being depressed is considered the same as admitting that they are crazy, so they
keep their personal problems to themselves. Older people
especially deny being depressed because they feel uncomfortable talking about feelings and other ''personal''
things. But we, the family, can readily tell that something
is wrong; we just don't know what. So we worry and
may, at times, even cause the depressed person to feel
even more depressed because of our worry.

In many cases it is the family who refuses to face the
possibility that a loved one is depressed. Everyone keeps
up the pretense as long as possible, creating unbelievable
strains on everyone involved and preventing the depressed person from seeking out the help so desperately
needed.

Depression is acted out in many ways when communication flow is blocked. Bulimia, once thought to be
solely a separate eating disorder like anorexia nervosa,
is now regarded by some specialists as a form of depression. In fact, numerous studies suggest that bulimia pa-

tients can be treated successfully with specific antidepressant medications. Depression is also a component of many other disorders, such as alcoholism and obsessive-compulsion disorder. It also is often one of the complications following a stroke. People with chronic pain and chronic illnesses also may suffer from depression. In addition, depression symptoms may actually mask physical illnesses. These should always be ruled out first through a complete physical examination.

Psychiatrist Eric Pfeiffer, Director of the Suncoast Gerontology Center, University of South Florida in Tampa, admits that detecting depression can often be very difficult. A depressed person's behavior may vary depending on whom he or she is with at a particular time. "Sometimes a depressed person can only carry out one role," Pfeiffer said. "That is, a man might function satisfactorily at work, but be nonfunctional at home. At the office, his co-workers think he's just fine. Yet his wife complains that he collapses when he gets home, sits in front of the television, never talking, and is negative about everything and everybody. The man's peers at work can't understand what the wife is complaining about."

When your parent is depressed

Struggling with a parent's depression is especially difficult because your own identity is threatened. You cannot function fully as an adult because the autonomy isn't there; you haven't been able to "fly the nest" because your parent's depression holds you back. Frustration and hostility may build.

"My mother is depressed, but puts up a front for her friends," Judy, a forty-two-year-old lawyer admitted. "My father died five years ago. About the same time, Mother had to move out of the big house we all grew up in because it's a two-story and she found it hard to climb so many stairs. But her condo is beautiful, and it's large enough for almost all her old furniture and other possessions. She still has Middy, the housekeeper who took care of my brothers and me when we were little, so she's not alone in the daytime. Dad left her well-fixed so she doesn't have any financial worries. She should be happy and enjoy her life. But she doesn't.

"Her friends think she is so brave and stoic. She 'allows' them to take her out and fuss over her. 'Poor Jenny,' they say, 'Isn't she doing well,' or 'Jenny's so strong. She's a pillar of strength.' And Mother smiles weakly at them.

"Well, at home the 'pillar of strength' crumbles. I drop in for lunch whenever I can, and usually she's still in bed. She claims she's exhausted. When I ask her what she'd like to eat, she shrugs and says it doesn't matter. She just can't seem to make any kind of decision. Sometimes she'll just sit and cry. 'I'd be better off dead,' she'll moan. 'You'd be better off without me to worry about.'

"It's gotten so bad that my brothers won't call or drop in to see her without my badgering them for days. Mother's so negative about anything they try to talk about that they just sit there like clams and then call me to say they refuse to go back. They're angry and frustrated and I can't say I blame them. I know this sounds dumb, but she's not acting like a parent. We want her to be proud of us and of what we've achieved, like Dad was, but she doesn't even acknowledge us as adults. It's like she's empty and we don't how to fill her or with what.

"She doesn't enjoy having any of the grandkids over for a visit either; she daily inventories her wide range of aches and pains; and she finds going out to dinner with us too much effort. 'I'll have Middy make me a little something,' she'll say in her poor-me voice. When I talk to her on the phone she speaks in a whispered monotone. Sometimes there are such long pauses between her words that I wonder if she's hung up.

"Although Mother's beginning to dress like a bag lady, she won't let me take her shopping for new clothes. When I bring something to her to try on, she says she's too tired. I don't know why I bother. Do you know what really drives me crazy?'' Judy said, with a catch in her voice. ''Her friends don't see any of this behavior. *I* say I'm worried that she's so depressed, and they don't know what I'm talking about. Why does she do this? I get depressed myself just thinking about it.''

Some adult children are not as persistent. They just disassociate themselves from the depressed parents as much as possible, in order to save themselves.

''Everyone in my family was depressed.'' Mark, a free-lance photographer, confessed. ''I knew at an early age that I was absorbing the family's depression. At fifteen years of age, I made a conscious decision to be different from my parents.''

''It wasn't that easy for him to change,'' interjected Diane, his significant other. ''I don't think Mark realized how affected he had been by his parents' depression. When he got a contract for a job, for instance, he never celebrated it. He wasn't conditioned to it, to allowing himself to be happy. What was even worse was that when Mark was depressed, he'd transfer it to me. It's something we've had to work on; still work on even now after so many years together. Thank goodness we can talk about it.''

When your spouse (or significant other) is depressed

Although a parent's depression can be overwhelming, as children must struggle to ''parent'' their parent, a spouse's depression is even more catastrophic. It takes a tremendous toll on the mate; indeed on the entire family, not only in the outlay of time and energy to care for the depressed person but also in financial and emotional costs. In addition, the care required for the person who is depressed means less time to care for the emotional, physical, and financial needs of the other family members, including yourself.

Depression changes the very fabric of your marital relationship. You (the "well" mate) must now care for your sick spouse. Your relationship cannot remain egalitarian if it once was, and if it was not, roles become even more reversed and, eventually, strained. You end up handling the family finances because your depressed spouse is too passive to keep up with bills, investments, and other financial planning. The family may have to rely on your income alone. You may have to do the shopping, cleaning, and child care as well. If your spouse suffers from bipolar depression (manic depression), you also may find yourself becoming a policeman with the checkbook and having to return items purchased during a manic phase.

Your social life begins to fall off because your spouse's depression makes it too much of an effort for him or her to get dressed or go out. Having company in is no longer an option because your mate either becomes easily irritated or withdraws, adding little to the conversation. Your world becomes smaller and smaller, and you and other family members become more isolated, causing you to begin to lose sympathy for the depressed person and to resent both the way the depression is enveloping the entire family, and possibly the depressed person as well.

At first it's natural to protect yourself and your family by ignoring your spouse's behavior. "I did that for a long time," sighed Suzanne, a woman in her fifties. "Then I denied anything was different. I made excuses. Nothing was wrong with Robert. He was just 'down' because business was bad. We own and operate a small dress shop in a shopping center and a new discount store had just opened up and undercut our prices. Business had fallen off. Who wouldn't be down?

"I figured it would pass. I decided that was why Robert seemed so distant and wasn't interested in sex anymore. We had enjoyed a good sex life before that—probably above average for people our age. Now he just collapses into bed. Not that he goes right to sleep. He doesn't. He tosses and turns so much I moved into the extra bed in our daughter's room. I guess that's upset him, too.

"I've tried to be understanding, patient, and caring—all the things a 'good' wife should do. But he hasn't gotten any better. I've suggested his going to a doctor, but he won't. He claims nothing's wrong. I'm getting discouraged.

"He sighs a lot, especially at dinner. Before he ate with gusto. Now he just picks. When I ask if anything is wrong, he just shakes his head and says, 'No.' I'll say, 'Well, business has to pick up.' But he obviously doesn't want to talk about it, and I guess I'm afraid to press the issue. I don't want him to start crying. It's awful when he does that.

"Needless to say, mealtime isn't much fun. Lisa and Joel, our teenagers, have stopped coming to meals, other than those when I almost command their presence. When they do, the silence is so thick you could cut it with a dull knife. It usually ends up with my talking to the kids and all three of us just ignoring Robert. He's become a shadow parent. Nothing interests him. When Lisa showed him some of her college catalogues he just nodded, but you could tell he wasn't very interested. Joel is hurt that his dad won't come to his basketball games. He's become someone we hardly know.

"Recently Robert's stopped going to the store and just sits home pretending to go over figures, but you can see he isn't even looking at them. We have a good manager, but with the new competition in the center, I'm not willing to dump the advertising and buying all on him. I've offered to go in to help, but Robert can't decide if he wants me to or not. Lisa said she'd forget about out-of-state schools and just concentrate on the state schools if that would relieve her dad's mind. He just shrugs and says it doesn't matter. He is maddening.

"At first I tried to be understanding. Now I'm angry. Nothing I do seems to matter. I've suggested his going to someone for help, but he doesn't think there's a real problem, and he doesn't believe in psychology either. 'I'm not nuts,' he says when I mention his seeing a therapist. Maybe he isn't, but *I'm* getting there. I've begun to become paranoid, thinking that he is doing this to spite me or something. I can see that his behavior is destroying our family. Our marriage, which I once thought inviolate, is shaky. I resent what he's doing. I know he probably can't help it, but why won't he get help? It's as though he doesn't care.''

Although Suzanne probably would have felt a similar sense of frustration and stress if her husband had suffered a stroke or had a chronic illness, depression tends to be more difficult to handle because we often feel embarrassed about it, as though there is some type of shame involved with suffering from depression. Part of this woman's anger comes from the fear we all have about any kind of mental illness. Some of that is due, I think, to our lack of understanding of what mental illness and, more specifically, what depression, really is. It also is caused by our worrying about what others may think when they hear someone in our family is suffering from depression.

I noticed reactions like this from friends and acquaintances who asked about what I was presently working on.

"Oh, it's a book about depression. What families should know about depression," I'd answer casually.

"Boy, I can relate to that," they'd answer.

"Really?" I'd respond. "If you've had some experience with depression in your family, I'd like to talk with you about it."

Often the person would look startled. They hesitated, mentally weighing the "risk" involved in sharing such potentially embarrassing material. Fortunately most people, when assured that their stories would be kept confidential and that I would alter ages, professions, and so on to disguise identities, agreed to share their experiences.

Families of the depressed are at risk

Depression can be extremely destructive, creating tremendous torment for both its sufferer and for those who care. It damages existing relationships and often nullifies opportunities for forming new acquaintances; it kills careers, dead-ends dreams, and throws family life into total chaos. In its most serious form, depression can drive its prey to suicide.

But the depressed person is not its only victim. Depression can spread through an entire family like a forest fire. According to Dr. Anne S. Lockey, a Tampa psychiatrist, "Usually mothers of depressed kids are depressed, too." The reverse, however, also is true. Children of depressed parents are more likely to become depressed than children whose parents are not depressed. Children with *two* depressed parents are four times more likely to become depressed themselves. The problems of depressed children are so immense that all of Chapter 10 is devoted to these issues.

It would be so simple if depression were caused by a germ and you could just give someone a pill or a shot to make it go away. Unfortunately it's not that easy. While some depressions do seem to disappear with time, most of them need to be treated—through changes in life-style and/or, by working with a professional—a psychiatrist, psychologist, family physician specifically trained to work with depressed patients, or other members of the "helping" professions, such as guidance counselors, religious leaders, or social workers who are fully trained mental health professionals—and, often, by taking advantage of specific medications and other forms of medical treatment.

You may look at the above paragraph and wonder, "What about me and the rest of the family? What about friends? Why can't we help make the depression go away?"

The omission was no oversight. As much as we love

someone, and regardless of how supportive we are both individually and as a group, a family cannot make one of its members happy or force them out of a depression. Neither can a best friend, no matter how well meaning. We can be empathetic; we can be supportive and caring. But we cannot *cure* someone of depression, no matter how hard we love them or want them to feel better.

Later chapters deal with specific ways in which you can help your loved one by being supportive and encouraging him or her to get and stay with professional treatment. Rid yourself right now of that overwhelming burden of guilt, the haunting sense that "if I only knew what to do, he'd snap out of his depression." He wouldn't and thinking that you did have the power to make things better would only serve to make *you* feel worse.

The causes of depression are controversial

Experts have difficulty in answering the question, "What causes depression?" There is no one right answer. It's hard to pin down what really causes depression because (1) there are numerous causes both in depression's transitory form as well as in its more severe form and (2) because situations and experiences affect people so very differently and in such varying degrees. They also affect a particular person differently depending on what else has gone on in his or her life at that specific moment. Researchers also are recently beginning to agree that there is a very real depression called "Seasonal Affective Disorder" (SAD), in which seasonality can affect and trigger mood disorders. In addition, some people may have a genetic vulnerability to depression.

In most cases, however, there are multiple factors that trigger a depression. A person may, in one circumstance, be able to stand firm and fight against the beginnings of a depression while at another time, such as after an illness or major loss, he or she may be more vulnerable and find it difficult, if not impossible, to "bounce back."

We, the family, may find it baffling and, at times, even irritating.

"Mother seemed to cope fairly well after my dad died," a middle-aged lawyer said. "She was sad and missed him because they had been close for fifty years, but otherwise she was fine. When her damned dog died, that was something else. She took to her bed and cried all day. She stopped eating and lost weight. It really hurt that the dog meant more to her than Dad."

More than likely this woman's dog *didn't* mean more to her than her late husband. It might have been that, to her, losing the dog meant that she was now truly alone. She might have managed through sheer determination to keep herself going after her husband's death, but losing her dog was the final blow to her own well-being. It also could be that other factors had changed in her life—her son and his family might have been moving away or having personal problems that caused her additional worry, her physical health might have deteriorated slightly, or there could have been a number of other different scenarios.

It's important to try to keep from being judgmental. Don't assume that because your aunt "was strong" when your uncle died that your mother shouldn't grieve so over your father's death, or that "plenty of men are forced into early retirement. Why can't you cope?"

Each of us is different. One woman may feel tremendous guilt over the fact that when her husband was ill with cancer, she sometimes wished he would die and get it over with. Another may have had the same thoughts but been able to accept that those were normal under the circumstance. Two youngsters are cut from the high school football team: one gets mad and is determined to build muscle and get into better shape the next year; the other goes home and shoots himself. Why? The answer is brutally brief: individual differences.

Reactive or Situational Depressions

Depression, like stress, is a part of life. Few people are so controlled that they go through life and seldom feel any highs or lows. Indeed, life would be rather bland were that the case. Almost everyone has mood swings. For some, however, the two ends of the continuum are fairly close together; for others, they are spaced widely apart.

In some cases, such as the death of a loved one, divorce, the move to a new city, or the loss of a job, being down, blue, and depressed are normal responses. In fact, we'd wonder if someone showed little or no reaction to these stressful life events. It's when the person can't seem to shake the blues, when the depression begins to take over the person's life for more than two weeks, causing passive behavior, prolonged sadness, loss of appetite, and a loss of a general zest for living, that he or she moves from being depressed to suffering from depression. Depression in cases such as this are called *reactive* or *situational* depressions; that is, they come in reaction to a situation, a specific event, usually one involving some change in a life situation.

"My father was always an upbeat type of person," a young architect said. "Then he was forced to retire because his company had a mandatory retirement age of sixty-five. Although he said he didn't mind, that he had all kinds of plans, the truth is that he felt lost. He became negative and angry. He said no one needed him anymore. Mother was busy with her church work and didn't want to give that up, although she tried to spend more time with him. But he began to make fun of her friends and belittled her church activities. 'Do-gooders,' he'd mumble at her.

"He drove all of us crazy. Everything he said was a put-down of something or somebody. He never had anything good to say. He wouldn't get involved in any volunteer work either. He just sat, alone, glaring at the outside world. Then he had a massive stroke. It's sad. He never did have the opportunity to enjoy his retirement."

Obviously everyone who retires doesn't become this depressed. There may be mild feelings of "What now?" or some sense of loss, but most people who retire are able to cope with this change of life-style and focus their interests in another direction. Possibly the gentleman described above could have adjusted to his retirement if other factors—a stronger self-image, specific plans and goals for post-retirement, closer peer network, comfortable financial situation, better communication skills, and so on—had been present. There also might have been unknown physical factors that precipitated his depression.

Other changes in life situation, such as having the last child go off to school or get married, may also cause depression. A mother who has lived her life through her children may now wonder what she will do with herself since she no longer feels needed. The father also finds his role changing, worries that it is proof he is growing older, and may fear living once again as a "two-some." Indeed, many seemingly happily married people who have not planned for this change in their life may suddenly look at each other as their last child pulls out of the driveway and wonder if they really want to spend the rest of their lives together now that the children are grown. Depression may set in and its passiveness hold both people captive for years.

Recent studies have also determined that people who have been victims of a violent crime such as rape, robbery, or physical assault may suffer from depression long after the actual event.

Depression also may occur in new mothers after a baby is born. Found in approximately one in ten new mothers, both those women who had planned their pregnancies as well as those for whom pregnancy came as an unwelcome surprise, postpartum depression (PPD) can be very frightening for family members as well as for the sufferer. The new mother—who need not be a first-time mother—may experience one or more of the following symptoms:

- crying for no apparent reason
- feeling certain that she has no natural motherly instincts
- having trouble sleeping
- developing dramatic changes in eating habits
- becoming either compulsive about the baby or ignoring it
- suffering from anxiety attacks

While an estimated 80 percent of women experience an emotional letdown after a baby's birth, known as "Baby Blues," that particular condition only lasts for a few days. Psychiatrist Madelaine M. Wohlreich, M.D., director of the Pennsylvania Hospital's Postpartum Disorders Project, suggests that any of the above symptoms lasting more than a few weeks goes beyond mere "Baby Blues," and may be cause for concern.

According to Dr. Wohlreich, "Postpartum depression usually begins two to six weeks after childbirth, and, if not treated, can persist for months or even years. But postpartum depression is highly treatable through short-term psychotherapy, medication, and other supportive measures. Many mothers who receive treatment recover within weeks.

"Unfortunately PPD is vastly misunderstood. The majority of women suffering from this condition do not recognize their symptoms as an illness or do not know where to seek treatment. They wrongly think that they are bad mothers."

If you think your family member may be suffering from postpartum depression, you may have to initiate action, as she will feel too helpless, worthless, or despondent to do so. Always seek qualified professional advice. The lay (nonmedical) organization "Depression After Delivery" can give you a list of women who have suffered from PPD in both the United States and Canada as well as support groups in or close to your area. They also publish a newsletter with information that might be of interest. There is a minimal membership fee for this material. Contact them at:

Depression After Delivery
P.O. Box 1282
Morrisville, PA 19067
Telephone: (215) 295-3994

Children may suffer from depression

As mentioned before, children—even infants—are susceptible to depression, too. Often they don't show the typical signs of depression that we see in adults. In many cases, a child's depression is "masked" and is acted out through the child's behavior. Depressed youngsters may show iistlessness and lack of concentration in the classroom, or they may go to the other extreme and become uncontrollable and hyperactive. They may destroy school property, become bullies and get into fights with other children, talk back to teachers, or otherwise upset classroom discipline.

Chapter 10 is devoted to the specific problems of childhood depression. If you have any concerns about your child's behavior, if you feel that he or she is withdrawn or moody, is beginning to do poorly academically, seems to lack concentration, or has become hyperactive and uncontrollable, read that chapter for more information. While these symptoms *could* be those of a learning disability or other problems, they also could be masking childhood depression. Don't ignore these signs of childhood depression, no matter how subtle. Childhood depression *can* lead to suicide.

Endogenous Depression

Some depressions seem to "come out of the blue" for no apparent reason. That is, they follow no specific known triggering event. This type of depression is called *endogenous depression* or *biochemical depression*.

Stedman's Medical Dictionary defines *endogenous* (pronounced: en-dodge-eh-nus) as "originating or produced within the organism." It's a fancy way of saying that this type of depression has a biological or chemical basis. This does *not* mean that a reactive depression is just "all in your head" as opposed to being "real," like the endogenous depression, however. Both are *real* depressions. Not only can the endogenous depression be just as debilitating as a reactive depression, but it also can be even more frustrating to families because with an endogenous depression there seems to be no apparent reason that triggered the depression. It just seems to come out of nowhere and envelop its victim like a fog. The most common symptoms of endogenous depressions are extreme fatigue (not relating to actual physical activity); headaches, with pain radiating to the neck; and lower back pain.

Manic Depression

Manic depression, now referred to as *bipolar depression*, is one form of endogenous depression. Although specific triggering events may be involved, the bipolar depression often forms a familiar pattern, such as recurring almost predictably at a certain season. Families and friends soon begin to recognize the signs that point to a manic state, such as when the person goes on almost continual shopping sprees, talks nonstop and goes for days with little or no sleep, or engages in a major physical activity in almost a frenzy, such as painting the entire house without stopping for meals or rest, writing voluminous notes for a project that often makes little sense, and so on.

This frantic activity may then be followed by a period of normality, which then changes into a deep depression during which the sufferer is exhausted, listless, and feels that he or she is a total failure as a person, that nothing can ever get any better, and that death would be a relief. Cycling time between extreme manic and depressive stages can differ greatly between individuals. Those who cycle back and forth from mania to depression without any "normal" periods are called rapid cyclers.

According to psychiatrist Dr. Eric Pfeiffer, this type of cyclical depression, or "bipolar depression," is extremely confusing to families because of the inconsistency of behavior and the knowledge that you really can't count on that person. "One day the sufferer may be on a 'high' and do everything with great gusto. The next day he can't get out of bed. The unpredictability is difficult for the family to handle."

Premenstrual Syndrome (PMS)

Experts suggest that anywhere from three to seven million American women suffer from depression resulting from premenstrual syndrome, a disorder linked to the hormonal system. While some physicians still tend to brush PMS off as "a psychological disturbance," the majority take it as a serious complaint and now treat it with a combination of hormonal, diet, exercise, and other therapies.

Seasonal Affective Disorder (SAD)

While it has been recognized for years that certain people tend to become depressed during the late fall and winter months, only to feel better as spring approaches, it is only recently that physicians have begun to accept SAD as a "real" disorder, caused, it seems, by a person's sensitivity to a hormone called melatonin, which is secreted by the pineal gland. Light supresses the secretion of the hormone while lack of light (as during winter) stimulates it. Doctors are beginning to treat these depressives by phototherapy; that is, by exposing them to special lights simulating the natural light of the sun with some success. While this procedure is fairly new, it may offer some hope to those who have recurring serious depressions in wintertime. The therapy does need to be carried out under a professional's care, however.

Illness and drug-related depressions

In addition to the above types of depression that arise from a particular episode or from biochemical causes, there is a third type. This type of depression typically follows specific illnesses or drug usage that includes prescription drugs, nonprescription drugs (including alcohol), and illegal drugs.

Stroke

It is estimated that 30 to 50 percent of all those who have suffered from a stroke become seriously depressed within the two years following the stroke. Some of the depression may be the normal result of the havoc created by the stroke. The patient becomes frustrated by the inability to do those things that he or she could do before the stroke, activities we all take for granted such as speaking, walking, feeding and dressing ourselves, and being able to think clearly. It's hardly surprising that the stroke patient is depressed.

But there is another side of the depression that follows a stroke, and it is thought to be an actual chemical change in the brain itself. Most strokes cause some degree of brain damage, either due to bleeding in the brain or by a blood clot or clogged arteries that cuts off the brain's oxygen supply. Certain brain cells are killed. This damage triggers a change in the chemical response in the brain that controls the stroke patient's emotional responses.

While the particular part of the person's brain damaged by the stroke does make a difference in regards to the severity of impairment, depression is always a possible side effect. Therefore, you should always remain alert for signs of depression—subtle or overt—following some-one's stroke.

Heart attacks, heart surgery, and chronic heart disease

Stroke is not the only illness that produces depression as a side effect. Depression, often serious depression, also is a common reaction for those who have undergone open-heart surgery or suffered a heart attack.

Some physicians feel that this type of depression is a shock reaction to the insult on the body's most emotionally-laden organ, the heart. That, and the fear of dying, may combine to trigger the depressive state.

Parkinson's disease, IBS, and other chronic disorders

Depression often affects those who are suffering from Parkinson's disease. Part of this may be chemically-based, shown by the fact that anti-Parkinson's drugs tend to improve the sufferer's mood. It also has an emotional basis, however, due to the progressively debilitating na-ture of the illness. Patients know that there is no cure for their disorder and that it will continue to cripple them, making them less functional and more dependent, until they eventually succumb. In addition, the muscular rigid-ity that comes with Parkinson's disease tends to force the facial muscles into a set expression that resembles some-one with depression. People tend to respond to that ex-pression as they do to anyone who looks sad and depressed, by withdrawing.

Irritable bowel syndrome (IBS), although a physical ailment, does not show up on X-rays or through other forms of diagnostic tests. But in trying to reassure their patients that their distress is nothing serious (e.g. can-cer), doctors often tend to minimize the complaint. Pa-tients then feel that the doctor thinks it is all in their mind, despite the fact that they continue to suffer from alternating constipation and/or diarrhea and cramps. Depression is a common reaction. As there *is* also an emotional component to disorders such as IBS, the depression only tends to make the person's discomfort worse, creating a frustrating and painful vicious circle.

Other chronic and more serious gastrointestinal disorders, such as Crohn's disease, diverticulitis, and ulcerative colitis, also can create depression in their sufferers, who not only feel crummy much of the time but also tend to withdraw from social situations because of the uncertainty and severity of their symptoms. This withdrawal forces them into isolation that only serves to accent their depression.

Rheumatoid arthritis, diabetes, hypertension, cancer, and multiple sclerosis are just a few of many additional chronic disorders that also have depression as one of their components. Two excellent books to help families deal with problems associated with chronic illness are *Mainstay* by Maggie Strong and *Meeting the Challenge of Disability or Chronic Illness—A Family Guide* by Lori A. Goldfarb, Mary Jane Brotherson, Jean Ann Summers, and Ann P. Turnbull.

Eating disorders

Although figures vary widely depending on which study is cited, an estimated 40 to 60 percent of women treated for eating disorders reported having earlier been treated for depression. In fact, many of the symptoms of depression—poor self-image, weight loss, sense of helplessness, repressed anger, and so on—are also symptoms of anorexia, bulimia, and bulimarexia.

Many bulimics admit that the depression that overwhelmed them after binging and purging was by far the most difficult side effect of their eating disorder, more upsetting to them emotionally than the constant dental problems, bleeding from the throat, and infected and swollen salivary glands caused by repeated vomiting and the effects of stomach acid in the mouth and throat. Some even consider suicide as the only way out of their eating disorder, without understanding or their family recognizing that depression is a major component of the problem.

Prescription drugs

Depression also results from many medications routinely prescribed for hypertension, anxiety, heart trouble, and weight loss (especially when the person has stopped taking the diet pills). Corticosteroids and birth control pills also may alter mood.

The elderly are particularly susceptible to reactions from medications because metabolism tends to slow down as we grow older. Prescription drugs are often given according to body weight, without factoring in this slowdown of metabolism or other factors specific to aging. Older people also may be confused, forget if they took their medication, and end up taking a second or third dosage. In addition, many senior citizens (and younger folks as well) often take numerous over-the-counter medications and fail to mention them to the doctor, figuring that they really "don't count" because they aren't prescription drugs. The truth is, over-the-counter drugs *do* count. Many of them intensify the effects of prescription drugs. In addition, many of them also contain alcohol, which is a depressant.

Remain alert to the number and types of over-the-counter medications your elderly parent or relative is taking. Write them down and compare with what others in the family have observed. You may be amazed when you inventory a family member's purse or dresser and virtually find a mini-pharmacy.

Alcohol usage

Alcohol, the drug used by many people to "wind down" after a busy day, is actually a depressant. As many people hedge when describing their actual alcohol usage to their physician, it's often very difficult for a doctor to know whether a depression is triggered by alcohol or some other cause.

Some of the over-the-counter "tonics" used by older people as well as younger people, including teenagers, also contain high percentages of alcohol. Even seemingly innocent over-the-counter cough syrups may contain as much as 43 percent alcohol (the same as 86-proof hard liquor). When combined with other drugs—prescribed and otherwise—these so-called "harmless" medications may induce depression.

If you have older parents, never assume that because you don't remember their drinking while you lived at home with them that they still do not. Many senior citizens turn to alcohol as a way to escape the unpleasant realities of the so-called "golden years," with friends dying, reduced financial means, their own aches and pains, and their mortality staring them in the face. Just as it's difficult for most of us to picture our parents having sex, it's difficult to imagine our parents, our children's gray-haired and loving grandparents, as heavy drinkers or alcoholics. But many of them are.

Illegal drugs

Some street drugs—like cocaine or speed—are stimulants. Ironically once their effect wears off the user is plunged into a physiological depression. Other illegal drugs such as marijuana are depressants.

Because street drugs are just that, chemicals compounded in filthy garages and empty warehouses to be sold on the street, there are no safeguards or actual standards. Drugs put into gelatine capsules by dealers only interested in dollars may vary drastically in strength or may be combined with other chemicals. By themselves—or even worse when mixed with alcohol—they can depress the nervous system enough to cause respiratory failure and death.

If you are middle-class, don't assume that street drugs could not be triggering a family member's depression, that it only happens to "the poor and disadvantaged." My community has a "Ride-Along" program, in which citizens are invited to ride along with a police officer to see first-hand what goes on when street drugs are being peddled. My officer told me that on Friday afternoons the known illegal drug areas are frequented by men and women in business suits—doctors, lawyers, CPAs, and other white-collar workers—driving by in expensive cars to buy their street drugs for the weekend. Just *my* community? Hardly. Unfortunately that scene is repeated far too often in too many cities, towns, and villages throughout our wonderful country.

Who gets depressed? All of us do sometimes in our life. The tragedy and disgrace is not in getting depressed or in having a family member who is depressed. The tragedy and disgrace is in keeping blinders over our eyes, pretending that depression doesn't exist, not in *our* family, and thereby condemning everyone—the depressed person and all the family to suffer needlessly. Depression can be controlled, but it needs to be recognized, accepted, and treated.

3

How You Can Recognize Depression

Everyone has times when they feel blue and apathetic, sometimes for no apparent reason and sometimes for very good reasons. I've felt down when my modern conveniences—the VCR, answering machine, and computer—stop working when I need them most, when it's rained for three days straight and the world seems gray, and when nothing in my closet fits; I've felt depressed when one of my kids wasn't doing well in school, when a publisher turned down a book proposal, and when I just felt overwhelmed in general. I've known despair when I was diagnosed as having cancer, when both of my parents suffered from strokes, and when my beloved younger brother died from cancer just last year.

Some of these depressed periods passed quickly, when someone (usually one of my kids) programmed the computer, answering machine, or VCR properly or when the sun came out and the world once again became blue and green and beautiful. Often depressions were lifted when I took some type of action, like finding a new (more enlightened) literary agent and losing weight or (more likely) buying some clothes in a larger size. But other despondent moods had no quick fix.

I couldn't change my cancer diagnosis; it was a fact. I had to accept the reality of a situation that made me both frightened and angry. I had to make certain decisions regarding my proposed treatment and then go on with my life. I handled the aftermath of my parents' strokes as best I could, mourning what could now never be for them and trying to make accommodations and arrangements for their present needs. I felt a powerful sense of sadness and loss as well as some regret for having to "grow up" and begin to parent them.

When my brother died, I was both numb and distraught. He was the baby in our family, the only boy. I had dressed him up and played with him like a doll when he was a toddler. I, along with a high school boyfriend who was on the wrestling team, had taught him to wrestle and win the forty-eight-pound championship for our YMCA when he was in grade school.

I had been his confidant, his friend, and his adoring sister when he reached manhood as well. His death left me feeling fatigued, drained, and terribly lonesome. I missed him. My hand still reaches for the phone to call him about some trivia or to tell him a joke. For months I wept often, in both private and public places—at the grocery, in a movie, and once at a business meeting. When a well-meaning acquaintance asked how I was, my throat tightened and tears filled my eyes. I found myself unable to speak. Ironically this person had lost both a sibling and a child and so unfortunately understood, but I was surprised by my lack of composure.

Yet I functioned. I completed a book (Strokes: What Families Should Know) ahead of deadline, went to all of my youngest son's baseball games, saw and enjoyed movies and plays. I was depressed, but I wasn't suffering from depression. Not then.

Depression had hit me over a decade earlier, suddenly and for no reason I could ever really pin down. It was before my malignancy was discovered; my parents were both still in good health and able to get around; my kids were doing fine in school; and my marriage was, as it still is at this writing, solid and rewarding.

Why then? What did I have to be depressed about?

Why would I have felt so down, so fatigued, so unsure of myself at that particular moment?

I really have no idea even to this day. I just know that at that point in my life I felt an unbearable sadness. I had no energy, no sense of urgency to do anything. I was passive. I'd find myself pulling the car into the driveway with no recollection of driving home. I'd sit in my study staring off into space, not thinking of anything, not focusing on anything in particular, my mind the proverbial total blank. Mail piled up as I opened only those that appeared to be bills and didn't bother to look at the rest, let alone throw the junk mail away. My joints ached; I felt totally exhausted, as though I had done a full day of heavy manual labor, when in truth I had done little other than to drag myself out of bed.

Discouraged by my internist's inability to find anything physically wrong with me, I went out of town, to a major clinic for a complete physical. After numerous tests they did find something wrong: I was suffering from depression.

What's the difference then? At what point should you be concerned about a family member's depression? When, in fact, does "being depressed" become "serious depression"? How *do* you tell when to get help for a loved one? How low is "too low"? When does so-called "normal" behavior become excessive and cause for concern?

When does "being depressed" become "serious depression"?

Most experts agree that depression should be of concern when:

- it interferes with a person's daily functioning
- when it continues over too long a period of time.

But how much interference is "too much" and how long is "a period of time"?

Unfortunately there is no litmus test to take that shows you when you should first become concerned about someone's depression. Depression is a continuum disorder. At one end are the blues and "blah" feeling you get on Monday morning when it's time to go back to work and you'd love to sleep in; at the other end, a feeling of such despair and weariness that it leads to the act of suicide. There is, of course, a great deal of variation in between those two extremes.

This diversity of mood that encompasses what we label depression is what makes the diagnosis so difficult and is why you need to bring in the experts. It's difficult for us as laypeople to recognize just how much of someone's daily functioning has been impaired, especially when the alterations in behavior are subtle or when we're busy with our own lives and don't notice gradual changes.

"My husband stopped shaving," one woman said simply. "Of course, many men decide to grow beards. But George always had been fastidious about his appearance. I should have been more aware of what was going on. He began to wear the same shirt two and three days in a row and often didn't bother to shower or wash his hair. The worst was that my once wonderfully optimistic and upbeat husband became terribly negative. He managed to find fault with everything—my cooking, the way the laundry did his shirts, his secretary, and even the way our dog barked. It wasn't until our daughter came home from school and commented on how different Daddy was that I focused on how much his former functioning had changed."

For some people the behavior displayed was once appropriate for the particular occasion but now they seem "stuck," locked into that particular emotional state. They withdraw from those around them; they lose interest in former activities; they *look* sad.

If a loved one dies, for example, it's expected that

family members will mourn, break into tears often and without provocation, and find it difficult to make decisions for a while. Yet most people basically still are able to function to some degree. In time—six months for some, a year or more for others—the numbness does wear off to a degree. You don't forget, but you go on.

But if someone you care for isn't able to shake off grief or other powerful emotion, if he or she always seems exhausted and sad or shows any other signs typical of depression so that you and the rest of the family are concerned, chances are it *is* a depression. You need professional help.

Dr. Anne Lockey suggests that if you think someone is showing changes in behavior that you think may be signs of depression, you need to begin to keep a journal, noting behavior, eating, and sleeping patterns; odd conversation; and anything else that troubles you. It may seem a little like spying, but it really isn't. Think of it more as taking notes to refresh your memory. The human mind is strange when it comes to measuring time. If you don't record what you see and hear along with your gut feeling, you may not realize how many weeks have slipped by. What you might think is only a couple of weeks may actually be four to five months when you begin to compare notes with the rest of the family.

"I didn't even realize that my father was depressed," admitted Matt, a forty-two-year-old advertising executive. "I was caught up with a new major account and going to my daughter's volleyball games, as she was the star of her team. I knew that Dad seemed tired and wasn't going out much, but it wasn't until my sister called and said, 'Hey, what gives? Every letter you've written in the last four months says that Dad seems beat or didn't come for dinner that week. When I've called his voice seems flat. Is he depressed?' that I started thinking back. When I did that, I suddenly became aware that he *was* depressed and that, even worse, it had been going on for a long time and it hadn't even registered on me."

This shock of "He's *still* doing that" is not unusual. George, a thirty-five-year-old salesman, was astonished to learn that his wife of the same age was seriously depressed. "She just slept a lot," he said. "She'd still be in bed when I left for work and took the kids to school. They'd come home, have a snack, and watch television, and she'd still be in bed. She'd get up when I came home, but usually she hadn't cooked anything for dinner, let alone done the laundry or cleaning. I just got mad. I thought she was lazy. It never occurred to me that she could be depressed. She never cried or seemed depressed. How was I to know?"

What are the specific signs of depression?

It's often difficult to know when someone's depressed. While you need to use your common sense and powers of observation to determine when someone you love may be suffering from depression, it's also important to learn and become aware of specific signs that signal depression.

The American Psychiatric Association has set up very specific criteria to be used to make the diagnosis of major depression. The following signs have been adapted from their guidelines:

1. Persistent mood of discomfort: depression, feeling low or irritable, showing signs of hopelessness, including a loss of interest in things and a loss of a sense of pleasure.
2. At least four of the following symptoms for at least two weeks:

• Poor appetite or weight loss (or increased appetite or weight gain)
• Change in sleeping habits, such as insomnia, waking up earlier, or hypersomnia (sleeping for long periods of time)

- Psychomotor agitation (such as pacing, sighing, or wringing hands) or motor retardation (slowdown of motions)
- Loss of interest in normal activities or decrease in sexual drive
- Loss of energy
- Feelings of worthlessness, inadequacy, or excessive (and inappropriate) guilt
- Reduced concentration or indecisiveness
- Suicidal ideation (thoughts of death or actual suicide attempts)

The criteria include the additional stipulation, ". . . if not otherwise imposed on schizophrenia or due to organic mental disorder or bereavement."[1]

Obviously use of the above criteria, which have been adapted from the American Psychiatric Association's *Diagnostic and Statistical Manual of Mental Disorders*, is based on your observations. It, therefore, is subjective. But trust your instinct. Don't censor your gut feelings. If you suspect a loved one is depressed, based on what you see and a knowledge of the above signs of depression, and it lasts for two weeks or more, there's a good chance that you are correct. Ask other family members to share their thoughts and concerns as well.

If your depressed relative is willing to answer a short questionnaire, ask him or her to complete the following "self-inventory" by first reading each group of statements carefully then answering the way he or she has been feeling within the past week. Check the answer in the appropriate column:

	always	*often*	*sometimes*	*never*
1. I feel exhausted.				
2. I feel sad.				

always   often   sometimes   never

3. I don't have
   much appetite
   or overeat.

4. I've lost
   interest in
   work, my
   hobby, friends,
   etc.

5. I get irritated
   easily.

6. I have difficulty
   making
   decisions.

7. I'm having
   trouble sleeping
   or sleep too
   much.

8. I have many
   aches and
   pains.

9. I'm not
   interested in
   sex.

10. I feel guilty and
    anxious.

11. I cry easily.

12. I wish I were
    dead.

Although this is a fairly unsophisticated quiz, more than two or more scores marked in the "always" or "often" columns may suggest a serious depression and need for professional help. (NOTE: If the response to "I wish I were dead," is "always," "often," or "sometimes," get immediate professional help. Contrary to myth, people who talk or think about suicide often DO try to carry it out.)

Remember, however, that a person can cheat on a questionnaire such as this and disguise his or her answers, giving the response that sounds most upbeat rather than one that matches true feelings. If your relative's behavior suggests to you or other family members that he or she is depressed, go by your instincts, not by a numerical score.

Despite your awareness of the specific criteria used for making a diagnosis of depression, a nonprofessional is never really qualified to determine whether or not a family member is depressed. Actually, it often is a difficult diagnosis even for a trained professional, as some people who are seriously depressed manage to show few signs.

Depression in the elderly is difficult to diagnose

Although it is estimated that between 10 and 15 percent of our elderly population is depressed, it is often difficult to diagnose. It's unlikely that you can ever get an elderly loved one to admit that he or she is depressed. Signs of fatigue are likely to be brushed aside with the words, "Well, I'm old. What do you expect?" When you express concern about weight loss, you'll probably hear, "It's too hot to eat. You know I don't have much of an appetite anymore." So chances are you'll back off, rationalizing that what you see are unavoidable signs of aging or worse of senility.

Detecting depression is also particularly difficult with this age group because they tend to regard any type of "mental weakness" as a stigma. That generation was raised, for the most part, to protect their emotions and "not air dirty linen." Trying to convince your parent or other older relative to see a psychologist or psychiatrist to talk about "personal" things may take some fancy footwork.

Sometimes what you see and consider to be depression really isn't. What may resemble symptoms of depression could actually be side effects of some of the various medications the person is taking for heart, arthritis, or other chronic conditions, or from the interaction of these many drugs. An older person's metabolism processes chemicals more slowly than a "normal adult," for whom the standard dosage requirements are set. That means a drug will stay in an older person's system longer. Gerontologists—physicians who specialize in older patients—and other doctors who treat elderly patients must take this into consideration when prescribing medication. Always inform the physician what medications—prescription and over-the-counter—your relative is taking.

An older person also may be suffering from other conditions that cause symptoms of depression, such as Parkinson's disease, Alzheimer's disease, or chronic pain. A number of years ago my mother-in-law took to her bed, exhausted, withdrawn, totally disinterested in food. She seemed depressed, although nothing particular had happened that recently in her life to trigger her depression (she had lost her husband thirty years before). She certainly wasn't under a great deal of stress. "It's senility," one physician said. "There's nothing you can do."

Fortunately we got a second opinion. This doctor specialized in endocrinology, the body's chemistry. After conducting various tests, he determined that her thyroid gland was not working properly. The imbalance of this particular chemical in her system had created a depressionlike stupor. Once she began taking pills to compensate for her malfunctioning thyroid gland, she recovered completely and lived ten more comfortable and happy years.

Many of the signs of depression—becoming easily fatigued, slowing down in speech and movements, reduction in appetite, change in sleep habits, and so on—are, on a lesser scale, part of the normal aging process. But it's so easy to write the behavioral changes off as "old age" and be fooled. According to an article in the Lahey Clinic Health Letter, "Traditionally, despondence in an older person has been attributed to an inability to cope with the realities of aging, such as diminishing physical abilities or the death of a spouse. But recent studies have increasingly pointed to physical and biochemical causes, including endocrine, neurological, cardiac and respiratory diseases, and the medications used to treat them."[2]

That's not to say, however, that an elderly person can't be "just" depressed. They can be and often are. But you have to be careful not to confuse someone whose arthritis forces him or her to move slowly, but basically is enthusiastic and interested in many things, with someone who moves slowly because motion of any kind is just too exhausting while he or she is bogged down in the quagmire of depression.

How to tell if your child is depressed

Although some adults may think of their childhood in idyllic terms and with fond memories, far more swear emphatically that they would never want to be a child again. Those supposedly carefree days actually, for most people, were filled with fears—both real and imagined—failures, and frustration.

Most of the signs of depression as described above, are, in various forms, part of growing from child to adolescent to adult. Uncertainty of identity, fear of separation from loved ones, lack of self-esteem, and guilt for everything from not living up to parental expectation to sometimes secretly wishing a parent or sibling was dead, are part of the evolutionary process of most young people.

How then is a parent to distinguish between the teenager who hides out in his or her room because of a need for privacy with one who is there out of loneliness? When should a child's zeal for perfectionism cause concern, not parental pride? How do you know when your youngster's actions—unruly behavior in school, alcohol or drug usage, or reckless driving—is really the acting out of depression?

It's tough. Children, especially those in their teen years, tend to be moody as they try different emotions on for size. They flirt with adulthood and demand privacy only to flee back into the security of childhood and your protection. It's tough on them and hard on you as well.

Although Chapter 10 discusses in depth what to do when your child is depressed, it's important first to learn how to recognize depression in your child and remain on a ready alert.

Although children may inherit a genetic vulnerability to depression, many childhood depressions are situational, created in reaction to one or more events. It may be difficult to understand why some things we as adults consider "minor" can be so devastating to a young person. We, of course, now can look back on those disappointments from an adult perspective and know that, although they seemed major at the time, they really, in retrospect, often weren't so important. We may have sustained far worse problems in our adult years and now know that we can cope with things that might have thrown us earlier, when we were less experienced with life and less certain of our own strengths. Now we probably understand that another job or relationship often does appear even though we were sure at the time none could be as perfect as the one lost. But it was and often it was even better.

For some, however, childhood losses may still hurt. "My father never really got over the fact that he didn't make the varsity football team in high school," Dave, a middle-aged man told me sadly. "Dad was captain of the J.V., but couldn't make the varsity, not even in his senior year. He's in his late eighties now, and I think that bitterness has kept him depressed all of his adult years. Throughout his life, he never felt equal to his older brother, who had made the team. He's had numerous major successes in many areas over the years, but none of them ever made him feel 'whole,' like a 'real man,' whatever that means.

"No," Dave said, before I could ask. "I never went out for football. I didn't want to compete with my father's fantasy."

How can you tell when a child is depressed?

Children who are depressed often don't look particularly sad. Some children may tell their parents or teachers that they're depressed, but most cannot. They may keep it buried, showing their depression through actions rather than words. You may have to sift through the silence, to hear what they aren't saying.

It isn't always that the youngsters don't want to tell you that they're upset. It's that they really don't know how or what words to use. Their vocabulary isn't fully functional yet, and they may feel uncomfortable trying to describe their feelings, unpredictable and intense emotions that seem to pop up out of nowhere, like the faces in a carnival's fun house.

For some young people the problem is more serious than the lack of proper words. These youngsters have grown up in a communication-deprived environment, where certain topics are forbidden. It's not that anyone ever said, "Hey, we don't talk about things like that." It's not that obvious. But a child is sensitive to subtle nuances and soon learns what is or is not permitted as conversation. This may be true in your house without your being aware of it. You may have learned the same lessons from your parents when *you* were a child.

You probably will have to determine whether or not your child is depressed by watching him or her at home and around other children and by being aware of the signs of depression in children and adolescents. To help you remember some of the signs of childhood depression, remember the acronym "IN SCALE." The letters represent the beginning of the first word of various symptoms of childhood depression.

I-Interest
A depressed child tends to lose interest in those things that previously seemed important to him or her. This is acted out by quitting a sports team or drama group that may have required great effort to join, by ignoring or just getting by with academic work, and by isolating him or herself from peers.

N-Negative self-image
Most young people normally have trouble with their self-esteem. They worry about not fitting into whatever the "perfect image" is that their particular peer group has conjured up. Thus, boys worry that they are too fat or thin, that their penis is too small, that their face is broken out, or that they'll never grow. Girls' self-image is usually no better. Girls worry that they're too tall or too short, too fat (even those who suffer from anorexia think that), ugly, have "funny" hair, a "strange" nose, no breasts or breasts that are too big, and so on.

It does parents little good to argue. If you say, "Your nose is fine. What's wrong with it?" your child will probably respond, "You're my mother. Of course you think it's great, but look at this bump!" Youngsters will stare at themselves in the mirror, hunting for the slightest blemish. When they find the very hint of a tiny pimple, they can be devastated.

It's really not that kids want to be perfect. But their self-image is just developing. They don't know *how* they feel about themselves or what to think. So they worry about their appearance because they can see that.

Depressed youngsters, however, carry this shaky self-esteem a little further. They consider themselves to be so unworthy, so lacking, that they feel nothing they do or say is ever right. They put themselves down constantly both vocally and through their actions. Their peers pick up through their body language that these youngsters don't consider themselves very important. Friends withdraw, and the depressed child is isolated just at a time when social contact is so very important.

Your child may display this lack of self-esteem in many ways, such as allowing you to select his or her wardrobe long after most youngsters are picking out their own, by always asking your opinion when faced with a choice of course electives or whether or not to go on a field trip, or by just shrugging when faced with options and saying it really doesn't matter. Listen to how your child refers to himself or herself and how any accomplishments are described. A depressed youngster will point out what wasn't good about a project, how it could have been done better, or how inept he or she is.

Depressed children tend to be passive because they don't feel worthy of making a decision, don't think anyone would be interested in what they think, and because it's just too much effort to be otherwise.

S-Sleep

Your child's sleep habits may change if he or she becomes depressed. Rather than quickly falling asleep, as most young people do, the depressed youngster may toss and turn or may fall asleep, but awaken early in the morning and be wide awake. This symptom is difficult for parents to detect unless the walls are thin and you can hear your child's restlessness, or if, less likely, he or she confides in you.

More observable is the youngster who can't seem to get enough sleep. While most normal teenagers can "sack out" until after noon on weekends, they awake refreshed and ready for activity. This is in sharp contrast with the depressed adolescent, who sleeps whenever possible and still seems groggy and lethargic when awake.

C-Concentration

Just like their adult counterparts, depressed children have difficulty in focusing. Their short attention span creates major difficulties for them at school because they process only bits of what's being said, miss instructions, and generally tend to drive their teachers into considering early retirement. Often, however, it is the teacher who first notices a child's possible depression and points it out to the parents.

Some depressed children tend to be accident-prone. It may be explained away by parents and siblings as attention-getting behavior or just an overly active youngster, but often the accidents are caused because of the child's lack of ability to concentrate or by a self-hate that flirts with potentially self-destructive behavior.

A-Appetite

The lethargy that comes with depression also affects appetite. Depressed children may lose their formerly good appetite and just pick at their food at mealtime. At school they may give away their lunches to others figuring, rightly so, that their parents will be none the wiser.

The depression may also express itself through eating disorders such as anorexia and bulimia. The youngster, usually a girl, will swear she is eating plenty despite the fact that she continues to lose weight. Regardless how observant parents may become, the child with an eating disorder may fool them, hiding food in her napkin, slipping it under the table to be eaten by the family dog, or camouflaging it to blend in with potato skins, bones, or other food left on the plate. The bulimic child will eat the food only to vomit it up again in private.

Some depressed adolescents treat food as an opiate for

their pain rather than something to ignore. These young-sters will gorge themselves, eating constantly, sometimes ransacking not only their own refrigerators but stealing food from groceries and open-air markets as well as from their classmates' lunch boxes.

L-Lost

This symptom of childhood depression is one you must observe subjectively. Your child seems . . . well, lost. He or she doesn't seem to have any direction and worse doesn't seem to care.

Your child may be frightened of many things or seem fearful to try the unknown. He or she may be a "wor-rier."

If you can imagine yourself a stranger observing your child, you might, without knowing anything about this child, nevertheless sense depression from the body lan-guage, from the expression of hopelessness and helpless-ness on the child's face.

E-Energy

This symptom is expressed through some of the others on the list, but it stands on its own because it's different from what you would expect. Kids are supposed to have endless energy. That's one of the reasons adults often say "youth is wasted on the young." They can burn the can-dle at both ends and would in the middle as well, if they could figure out how.

But a young person who becomes depressed doesn't have this energy. He or she seems bored with the world. Everything seems to be too much of an effort. "I'm tired," is the complaint.

Naturally your first step is always to arrange for a phys-ical examination to be sure your youngster isn't suffering from poor nutrition, inadequate physical conditioning, mono, or a number of other physical disorders.

Thoughts of death or suicide

This sign of depression doesn't fit neatly into the acronym IN SCALE. It doesn't need to. It must stand on its own because it is such an important one to remember. Children who seem preoccupied with thoughts of death and dying or of suicide are probably depressed. Many depressed young people do attempt suicide, and, most tragically, many of them succeed. Suicide is always a concern when anyone is depressed. For this reason, please read chapter 13, which deals with the symptoms of a suicidal person and what you can do to help.

Some experts include "masked" signs of childhood depression with the above. These signs are behaviors that are expressed in place of what we think of as typically depressed behaviors. They include:

Aggressive behavior

Rather than being withdrawn, which is what we expect to find in a depressed adolescent's behavior, some youngsters will become overly aggressive, starting fights on the playground and in the gym, talking back to teachers and parents, and defying authority in general. This is the Jimmy Cagney-type "tough guy" who acts like he has a chip on his shoulder but inside may be desperately hurting and afraid. This type of depression is often hard to detect because he tends to make everyone—parents, teachers, and others in authority—so angry that it's often hard to look beneath the bully's behavior.

Psychosomatic illness

Perhaps you remember being sick and getting to stay home from school and having your mother all to yourself. She brought Jell-O, lightly buttered toast, and chicken soup in her best china bowl to you on a tray so you could eat in bed; let you have the little television set in your room; and even made your older sister take out the garbage because you were too sick to do your chores. Ah, such bliss.

No wonder many children learn early that they can gain attention and be rewarded by being sick. For the depressed youngster, complaining of vague distress— headaches, stomachache, pains—is a ''safe'' way to express depression. It brings comfort and attention until those in authority—mother or school nurse—get tired of all the complaints.

While it is always important to check the complaint out with your pediatrician to be sure you aren't ignoring a stomachache that turns out to be a real appendicitis or ulcer, be alert to signs that your child may be becoming a hypochondriac and using pretend hurts to hide the ache of a real depression.

Hyperactivity

As mentioned above, most children who are depressed lack energy. They are listless, as though they were trying to conserve energy.

For some depressed youngsters, however, the opposite is true. These young people mask their depression through a whirlwind of activity. Anorexics spend countless hours exercising to burn up the few calories they have consumed that day. Others get up and wander around the classroom, unable to sit still or to concentrate. These may be the kids who mumble or hum to themselves while someone in authority is speaking, who blow bubbles, drum with their fingers on the desk or table, tap their feet in the movies, and otherwise are pictures of perpetual motion. It's almost as though they feel that by keeping on the move they can keep depression at bay. But they can't.

According to Dr. Joseph Lupo, depressed adolescents may act out their depression through risk-taking—jumping off fences and bridges or driving cars and motorcycles recklessly. They may engage in promiscuous sexual behavior, not because they are ''oversexed'' but because they are depressed and hurt and hope that through their behavior they may find relief from their pain. Often, sadly, the result instead is more pain—an unwanted pregnancy or sexually transmitted disease.

Many parents assume their child is "a little hyperactive" and don't consider any of the other options, one of which could be childhood depression. There *is* a specific condition called "hyperactivity" in which a child is restless and has difficulty concentrating. How can parents determine whether their child is suffering from depression or from the hyperactive condition? The truth is, they cannot. Only a professional is trained to tell the difference, and even they often must rely on specific tests to help them make the diagnosis.

If you have any concerns or doubts about whether or not someone you love is suffering from depression, or even whether or not a depression is serious enough to require treatment, always seek qualified help. Remember, depression can be fatal; it can end with a successful suicide attempt.

Endnotes

1. Adapted from American Psychiatric Association, *Diagnostic and Statistical Manual of Mental Disorders. Third Edition, Revised.* (Washington, D.C.: American Psychiatric Association, 1987).
2. "Depression in the Elderly—Complex but Treatable," *The Lahey Clinic Health Letter* (Burlington, MA), April 1990.

4

Why Is Depression "Catching"?

Few people would deny that colds and flu are infectious diseases. "It's going around" is the general excuse everyone—from your doctor to your best friend—makes when you begin to show signs of one of these ailments. Does it surprise you to know that depression spreads just as rapidly, and that like these other medical conditions depression, in its worse scenario, can also be a potentially fatal disorder?

Although researchers disagree to some extent on *why* depression is contagious, they all agree that it is. You don't need experts, however, to tell you that. If you love someone who is depressed, you've experienced that for yourself.

Aleen, a thirty-five-year-old housewife, described what it was like for her:

"I'm not embarrassed to admit that I'm basically a happy person. Life's been pretty good to me. My husband and I still love each other after twelve years of marriage, we have two kids who are terrific, and I enjoy the volunteer work I do in my kids' school. I think life is great . . . until I go to visit my parents who live in the same town as me. It's what the kids call a 'real downer.'

"My father talks about how terrible the world is, how everyone is out to screw you, how nothing is like it was when he was young. Mother is wrapped up in taking a

54

daily 'body count' of her aches and pains, which always are many. She could keep an entire medical clinic busy all by herself. Some of her pains, I admit, are very real. She has arthritis and her hands are pretty crippled up. She also can't see well out of one eye and is getting cataracts. Basically, however, for their age both of my parents are reasonably healthy.

"When I'm there for more than an hour I find myself feeling tired, angry, and, what's worse, even agreeing with them that life's the pits! I don't know what happens. It's like a horrible spell comes over me, and I absorb their depression in through my pores. I can't wait to get away. I find myself making up excuses to keep from paying a visit. My husband can tell when I've been with my parents because I'm down and blue for the rest of the day."

At least this woman is able to leave after visiting her depressed parents. For those living with a depressed family member under the same roof, life is more difficult and leaves family members in danger of becoming depressed as well. In fact, experts feel that those living with a depressed person have an *80 percent* chance of becoming depressed themselves.

Stress lowers resistance to depression

Mental health experts who deal with depressed youngsters say that these children often have depressed parents, but they fail to determine if the parents' depression triggers depression in their offspring or if having a depressed child triggered the depression in the parents. Certainly the strain and worry of having a depressed child can create tensions in any household and in any marriage. It also makes it difficult to reach out to your child who—though suffering as well—is nevertheless frustrating you and causing you to feel less than effective as a parent. You're bound to feel angry, resentful, and anxious as you look for something or some person to shoulder the "blame."

Other types of stress can make someone subject to depression. Perfectionists, those who demand no less than perfection from themselves as well as others, create stressful situations for themselves and their families. Since perfection is a difficult if not impossible goal to attain, the perfectionist sets himself up for failure and its close companion, depression. A parent who demands perfection from a child also sets too high a standard, creating heavy stress on a youngster who at the same time must struggle with the quest for self-image and a feeling of worth.

Stress is created from any new situation—changing schools, moving to a new neighborhood or town, a promotion at work where you're not too sure of yourself, and adjustment to changing family structure through divorce, marriage, a new baby, illness, or death. All these experiences can trigger a depression that spreads from one family member to the other.

Although we all have our own personalities, children do learn how to handle stress and new situations by watching how their parents react to them. The parents who take on a move to a new town as an adventure or exploration create a sense of fun and curiosity in their children; those who complain and mourn leaving friends, family, and familiar patterns behind may find their youngsters mimicking their actions.

Family fallout

When one family member becomes depressed it changes the entire functioning of a family unit. In addition to stress, mentioned above, there is a sense of loss, which not only may make you and the rest of the family feel sad and depressed yourselves, but also conjures up some guilt, anger, and resentment. You may not recognize or admit to these emotions. Even if you do, you may not want to deal with them. But they are there, and they are normal.

You and the rest of the family will find yourselves having to fill voids left by the depressed person. The comfortable and familiar family format that seemed to function in the past must now change. New roles must be cast, new reactions learned. It is an awkward time, like a junior prom where no one really wanted to be, but felt forced to show up. And like that near-forgotten prom, no one now knows for sure who's leading.

When your spouse is depressed

If the depressed person is your spouse who now finds it too difficult to continue working, you may have to get a job (or second job) to bring in income to compensate for his or her inability to work, or to provide additional funds to pay for medical care expenses or functions no longer carried out by the depressed person. You may need to find replacements for child care, and require assistance with carpooling, housework, and so on.

Your former life structure may change as well. You find less time for personal exercise and volunteer work because you feel you're needed at home. Your social life may suffer as friends, sensing your spouse's depression, pull away to protect themselves. It's not a lot of fun to be around a depressed person. You know that. Friends know that, too, but *they* don't have to be there. Without meaning to hurt, they just subtly make other plans for the weekend, get other bridge or tennis partners, and as they leave one by one, your circle slowly and painfully becomes smaller and smaller.

You and other family members are forced to face more time in isolation, alone with the depressed person. Any plans you may devise for recreation or pleasure may be rebuffed by someone so depressed that nothing seems fun or remotely enjoyable. You spend week after week in front of the television screen. Of course you resent it. It hurts. You feel unwanted. Your self-image has been shattered. You're lonely, and everything in your life that once sparkled seems covered by the dust of depression. Before you are aware of it, you, too, begin to feel depressed.

When your parent is depressed

If the depressed family member is your parent, you will find yourself handling additional responsibilities as you care for his or her personal needs, assist with financial matters, and try to provide even more emotional support when you feel in need of some yourself.

It's hard to juggle all you have to do in your life. Your work concentration is shattered when your father calls, weeping, to say he's no good for anything anymore, and you're torn between finishing with your client and running to your car to drive over to check on him. Your time with your spouse and children becomes fragmented with visits, errands, and endless telephone calls to reassure your mother that you do care about her aches and pains. Your ''private time'' when you used to enjoy walks, racquetball, or painting seems nonexistent or if used seems almost a selfish indulgence. Your guilt index rises to danger levels.

If you're a young person, having a parent suffer from depression is even harder. You keep trying to make your parent happy, but everything you do seems to lead to failure. You find your depressed mother or father leaning on you at a time when you feel *you* should be getting an assist. You grow up fast because someone has to make decisions, and your parent is so depressed that he or she is unable to. You drop out of sports, drama, or other school-related activities because you hate to be away from home so much and leave your parent alone. You find yourself playing parent to your parent. It probably doesn't make you feel grown-up at all. More than likely it makes you feel scared. You doubt yourself; you resent your parent. You curse your luck and ask why *you* have to have a parent who is depressed. Every young person you know seems to have wonderful, mentally healthy and supportive parents. It makes you sad and, yes, it makes you depressed.

When your child is depressed

A depressed child also can upset the family functioning. Although there may not be as many dropped responsibilities to assume, there are additional time commitments, as you meet with school officials to try to come up with plans to help make your youngster happy again, to discuss discipline for the youngster who is acting out a depression through unruly behavior, to take the child to medical appointments, and try to smooth problems over so "things can go back to the way they were."

Friendships also can falter when your child is depressed. You find yourself becoming self-conscious when friends ask how your child is feeling or press for information about what *really* is wrong. Laughing with friends about your child's preteen antics or teenage foibles is one thing, but admitting that your child is depressed is another. It makes you feel both apologetic and defensive. You'd never admit it, but you're embarrassed about this "depression thing." You tell your spouse it must come from his or her side of the family.

When your child's depressed, you find that it's easier to make excuses for not joining friends for dinner or a movie than to worry about what they'll say and what lies you'll make up to protect your youngster. You exhaust yourself dreaming up alibis to protect your child and the family and, of course, yourself. "What would others think?" you worry as you weave your web of deceit.

You worry about what caused your child to change; you worry about the effect of the depression on your other children and on your marriage; and you worry that your child might "do something stupid." (You can't bring yourself to even mention the word "suicide," despite the fact that suicide is the third leading cause of death among adolescents in the United States.) If you aren't careful, you and your spouse also may begin blaming each other for something that might have triggered your child's depression. You're too worried and too tired to realize that you have become tainted with depression as well.

Most of us feel drained and upset when we argue with our children, but at least arguing usually gets problems out in the open where they can be dealt with. Parents of depressed children say it is far more frightening when a youngster withdraws beyond reach because, as one mother put it, "I feel so incompetent. It makes me feel that *I'm* doing something wrong with him and that I'm too stupid to know how to make contact. It embarrasses me to admit I can't handle my own child. Then I start attacking myself for being such a lousy mother which, of course, results in my becoming depressed as well. My self-esteem is a minus ten."

When your sibling is depressed

Siblings also often suffer when a brother or sister becomes depressed. Children have a tendency to feel all-powerful. They may become angry and wish that their sibling would "get sick and die." If that sibling becomes depressed—either withdrawing from friends and family, becoming hyperactive and uncontrollable or, tragically, committing suicide—the other sibling may be tormented by the fear that he or she caused the illness. Not wanting to admit such a horrible deed to parents, the youngster may keep all the guilt inside and eventually become depressed as well.

"I knew my brother was depressed," Peter, a college professor, told me over lunch as he recalled his troubled boyhood. "I tried to be supportive, but it wasn't easy. One evening we sat out in back of the house. He was leaving for college later that night, but he really didn't want to go. He started talking, about real things for a change, about his thoughts and feelings. We kept getting interrupted by either the telephone or the other kids. Finally our father came out to tell him it was time to leave. He just gave up. When I tried to bring him out again, he just shrugged and left. Later that week, he tried to commit suicide. We've never discussed it since. I always felt I should have made him keep talking. I've carried that guilt for years. We aren't close anymore. In fact, I haven't seen him in years.''

Siblings of a depressed child may feel that they have been left to fend for themselves, that their parents are giving too much time and attention to the depressed one. The ''well'' children may resent this loss of parenting and may unconsciously adopt the depressed child's way of reacting to life in order to regain some attention from the parents.

There's also an element of embarrassment to a young person when a sibling ''acts like a jerk,'' as one teenager told me. ''I hate it when my grandparents come over because all they talk about is my sister and why she cries and hides in her room all the time. She is such a pain. I can't stand to be around her. I won't bring my friends over because I don't want them to see her.'' He admitted that he wished his sister would be like she had been. ''I miss having her to talk to,'' he muttered, his eyes filling with tears. Then he shook his head. ''Boy, is she strange now.''

This embarrassment of having a depressed sibling may back a youngster into isolation from friends to keep from being teased or from having to make explanations for the sick sibling's behavior. His or her fragile self-esteem may take a dip as well, especially if the depressed person was an older, much-looked-up-to sibling.

There's also the element of fear that comes from a lack of knowledge and misunderstanding what depression is. The youngster may worry, ''If it happens to my brother (or sister), can it happen to me as well?'' The answer, of course, is that it certainly could. This youngster truly becomes a child at risk and may be vulnerable to the same set of circumstances that triggered the depression in the other family member.

Unfortunately such a child often feels unable to communicate his or her concerns to a parent or teacher and certainly would not reveal his fears to a peer. The isolation becomes more intense and can pull a child into a depression as certain as the ocean's undertow can capture the imprudent swimmer.

Some things do not get better with age. Adult siblings are not immune to pain caused by an adult brother or sister's bout with depression either. They often experience the same sense of embarrassment and loss. "I get depressed when I think how my sister used to be compared to what she has become," said one middle-aged woman. "As a young girl, I worshipped her. She was the 'pretty one,' while I was just 'cute.' She could put together this blouse, that skirt, an old belt, and a scarf and come up with a fantastic outfit. I had no clothes sense at all. I always thought she looked like Elizabeth Taylor. She really was beautiful. Then, in her forties, she became severely anorexic and bulimic. I know now that she's clinically depressed and needs help, but she denies anything is wrong and refuses to get it. My knowing doesn't make it easier. I mourn the sister of my memory. I don't like looking at her or touching her. I just feel sad when I'm around her. It makes me depressed to see her looking like someone from a concentration camp. I make excuses to stay away."

While few of us would be embarrassed to admit to having a family member with a heart condition, diabetes, high blood pressure, or any other physical disorders, many people still feel shame at having a loved one suffering from a mental disorder such as depression. They go through extreme charades and waste valuable energy to cover up its existence, even to the point of making elaborate dinner plans with friends knowing that the date, most likely, would have to be canceled when the depressed person complained of being too tired, sad, or was just unable to get moving enough to go.

The depth of this deception and denial of depression

is surprising in this era of openness, when everyone's personal life seems to be an open book and we know everything about our movie heroes and television stars as well as about our political candidates including their problems with hemorrhoids.

Some people even resort to elaborate cover stories to protect their family member's problem with depression. Michael, a prominent attorney, whispered confidentially to me at a social function that his wife really didn't have hepatitis as everyone had been told. She was suffering from a serious depression, he said, and she hadn't left the house for weeks. He didn't want anyone to know but was sharing it with me because he had heard I was writing a book on depression.

I knew his friends had worried about them both because Michael looked so depressed himself that they all assumed his wife was critically ill; they didn't know that Michael had gone to such extremes to deny the existence of his wife's depression that he, too, was beginning to suffer from it.

Empathy makes you more susceptible to depression

Have you ever sat in a movie theatre or watched television and noticed the faces of those around you? When the actors are sad, the audiences' faces often reflect that emotion; when the characters are frightened, the members of the audience (if it is a good film) tend to open their eyes and wrinkle their faces to reflect the fear the actors are experiencing.

When a person is depressed, his or her entire body reflects it. The facial muscles sag, the corners of the mouth turn down, the eyelids tend to lower. The depressed person's shoulders droop. This expression is what we tend to think of as "a depressed look," or "sad sack expression." Actors and artists study this body language and use it to portray particular feeling. Good actors can suggest emotions just by the way they carry their body and alter their facial expressions. Without saying one word, they can make us feel their despair and hopelessness.

Although none of us likes to consider ourselves a copycat, the truth is we do tend to pick up on a person's body language and expression. If we're constantly surrounded by depressed people, it's most difficult to remain cheery. Often without our realizing it, we begin to imitate their body cues, subtly at first, then more obviously. We unconsciously copy their slowdown breathing patterns and even find ourselves sighing. What may have begun as a glorious day where we woke up singing—well, all right, we woke up in a good mood—now has turned gray and dull and to our amazement we actually feel depressed and wonder why.

I asked one psychiatrist that I interviewed if his practice consisted mostly of depressed patients.

''Good Lord, no,'' he exclaimed. ''I'd get depressed myself. You can't just be around depressed people.''

''Isn't that what happens to a family when one of its members is depressed?'' I asked.

He looked at me thoughtfully, then nodded.

Genetic disposition

Although there seems to be a genetic basis for bipolar depression, it is more probable that the *vulnerability* to reactive depression and endogenous depression tends to run in families. That means, you may be more likely to suffer from depression than someone with no disposition to it, but it does *not* mean that you will necessarily suffer from depression just because a parent, uncle, or grandparent did. It is possible, however, to experience depression as a learned response to stress and situational circumstances.

Later, in other chapters in this section, you'll find specific ways to deal with this circle of depression as well as tips on how to protect yourself from getting caught up in it.

5

Why You Must "Accent the Positive"

In 1952 a Methodist minister named Norman Vincent Peale wrote a bestselling book entitled *The Power of Positive Thinking*. It was just one of many motivational books written by this exceptional world-renowned speaker and author. They all contain the same theme: "Positive thinking can help you to maintain an upbeat attitude."

Numerous other books have been written since then by many other writers, all on the same principle, and a great number of them have become popular. Why have so many similar books become bestsellers? Because people desperately want to know the "secret of happiness." It's too simple just to "accent the positive," they think. There must be something more complex, some long list of rules to follow, perhaps, like the rainbow leading you to the pot of gold. But it really is that simple. Positive thoughts *do* make you feel happier. How do I know? Because I practice my own advice.

Why a chapter on "happy thinking," as one of my kids calls it? Because it's one of the best defenses against catching your loved one's depression. Remember the symptoms of depression: a sense of overwhelming hopelessness, loss of joy or sense of pleasure, loss of energy, and so on. All those symptoms equate sadness and lack of joy. To keep from absorbing them from someone who's depressed, you need to "inoculate" yourself with joy, to allow laughter in your life.

But it's difficult. You don't feel much like laughing while someone you love sits in another room crying or staring at the wall. How can you immerse yourself in pleasurable activities, while he or she won't even get dressed to go out of the house? It makes you feel guilty to enjoy yourself when someone you love feels so low. Are you being nonsupportive? Unfeeling? Selfish?

No! No! No! Every mental health professional interviewed for this book stressed the importance of the nondepressed family members making time for themselves, to be with other people, to laugh, and to enjoy life. It allows you to remain healthy both emotionally and physically, and makes you better prepared to care for someone who is depressed—more importantly, someone you love who is depressed.

According to Dr. Eric Pfeiffer, "Families of a depressed person MUST have lives of their own. If, for example, a wife is dependent on her husband to say how wonderful she is, her self-esteem will go down the drain if he becomes too depressed to bolster her."

NEVER underestimate the amount of physical and emotional energy you expend and will expend when you care for a depressed family member. It can suck you dry if you aren't watchful. You'll ride a roller coaster of emotion, drained one day, lulled into thinking "things are better" the next, only to be bumped into discouragement again the following. It's a long ride, so you need to be prepared.

Not only is there a tremendous emotional and physical investment when you're dealing with someone who is depressed, but there also is an amazing outlay of time, that most valuable resource that remains constant for all of us—just 24 hours each day, 168 hours each week. No matter how well you plan things or how organized you may be, when you're dealing with someone who is depressed you'll probably find yourself always behind schedule, always late. Unfortunately most "tips for time management" books don't include chapters that tell you how to deal with a depressed family member.

You'll have to start thinking in terms of slow motion, like movie scenes filmed with a slow-motion camera. The depressed person moves slowly, speaks slowly, and thinks slowly. (A bipolar depressive in a manic cycle, on the other hand, is just the opposite.) But someone who is depressed cannot be rushed. Your standing impatiently first on one foot then another only serves to create more stress, more depression, more feelings of hopelessness, along with the weary and dreary thought, "they'd all be better without me."

Dr. Pfeiffer stressed, "When someone suffers from bipolar depression, it is even more difficult for family members. You really can't count on him because you don't know what mood he'll be in. One day he'll be scurrying around, working with great gusto, while the next day he can't get out of bed. This uncertainty makes it hard for the family to bear."

Chapter 9 will give you specific tips on how to determine your physical and emotional limits and maintain your priorities to help you cope with this slowdown so you don't react with frustration, anger, additional stress, and depression of your own. You will, however, find yourself more able to maintain a positive attitude if you remember the following suggestions:

Accept the reality

There's no use sticking your head in the sand and pretending that nothing's really wrong with your family member. Face reality, and in terms of preserving your own sense of well-being, the fact that things *do* take longer and that there's nothing you (or your depressed family member) can do about that right now. The depression has taken hold and is in charge. What you may consider to be the simple tasks of taking off a nightgown or paja-

mas, putting on first underwear, and then shirt and
pants, not to mention socks and shoes, may seem not
simple, but rather a full day of activities to a depressed
person. Don't expect it to be different.

You'll also be happier if you accept the reality that it's
possible—through time, treatment, and medication—for
your loved one to get over a depression. Most people do.
While it's also true that a large percentage of those with
depression may suffer from it again, for today just focus
on today, and take life one day at a time. Don't worry
about the "What ifs . . ." They have the capacity to
overwhelm anyone, especially those who are struggling
to cope with a loved one's depression.

Allow extra time for tasks

Give yourself additional time so you don't feel pres-
sured. You know, for example, that getting your father to
the doctor is going to be a major production to him, so
make time for it. Even if you're just dropping him off
somewhere so another family member can take him, accept the reality that he's not going to just throw on his
coat, skip down the sidewalk, and hop into the car as he
used to. The depression has slowed things down, and
there's no use trying to rush him. You'll just upset yourself and possibly him as well. If you try to rush him, he
may just sit down, too overwhelmed to do anything.

Time, of course, is probably the one commodity you
are shortest on at this point. Most family members of a
depressed person are busy doing what they normally do
in addition to handling the ill person's tasks as well. You
may have found yourself taking on more and more responsibilities, picking up the slack when your loved one
just stares for hours at the checkbook or weeps that there's
nothing for dinner because it was just too much effort to
go to the store.

That's when you need to reassess priorities (see Chapter 9) and ask for help. There's no more shame in having

someone in your family who is depressed than in having a family member with a broken hip, cancer, or any other physical disorder. You need help, and it's there if you know where to look and if you are willing to ask. Those are two very important "ifs," and your happiness can depend on them.

Evoke the senses

Don't be afraid to show happiness around your depressed family member. You'll probably get little or no response, but *you'll* feel better. Enjoy nature. Comment on the warmth of the day, the beautiful cloud formations, or even the scent of flowers or the smell of fall in the air. Breathe deeply. Smile. Perhaps, if you're lucky, your loved one will return a little, though somewhat pathetic, smile in return.

But don't worry if you get no reaction or even if he or she starts crying. Depressed people can't control their emotions. The tears may be in frustration or possibly even in joy, though it cannot as yet be expressed.

Your loved one may seem totally indifferent to the beauties of nature that you point out. It's not being contrary, but that the depression creates a sense of indifference to surroundings, people, or events. A sunset that you think is the most glorious ever seen by mankind may pass without a comment by your depressed family member even if he or she was the one who used to make you stop the car to watch the sun set before the depression took hold. Your description of mouth-tempting foods may get no reaction, even from a former gourmet; those with depression usually have little appetite or interest in food. (Those depressives with eating disorders are the exception. Even anorexics, who seem close to starvation, are usually preoccupied with thoughts and conversation centering on food and take great delight in fixing elaborate meals for their families, even though the anorexic does not permit herself to taste even one bite.)

Nevertheless, it's important for *you* to keep exercising your senses—touch, taste, sight, smell, and sound. They're dulled for depressed people, and if you don't make an *exaggerated* effort to use them to bolster your own mood, they'll gradually dull for you as well. You'll find that soon you don't really care if the food's bland or not, that you don't hear the birds chirping, and that the smell of freshly baked bread doesn't make your mouth water. So use it, even accentuate it, before you lose it.

Make time for you

You'll be much happier and depression-free yourself if you take time for yourself, to do those things that bring you pleasure and comfort. The following three chapters deal with specifics on what you can do—exercise, relaxing, becoming assertive, and so on—to make you feel better, but you will only put those ideas into practice if you first believe that it is okay for you to be happy and that you are entitled to having some time for yourself. That includes time to be alone with your thoughts, to exercise, to listen to music, paint, or do whatever it is that brings peace to your soul.

It also means time to be with others who are not depressed, not in order to leave your family member in isolation but rather to free you from the isolation that comes when you are living with a depressed person. It means finding and maintaining friendships with those who are upbeat, who love life, who find joy in the little things you've almost forgotten.

You need your friends, not only to act as a sounding board, listening to you as you blow off steam, but also to help you focus on happy topics, to remind you that most of the world is *not* depressed, and that you need to remain positive so you don't get caught up in a depression as well. Be careful, though, not to treat your times with friends as merely recital time for all your gripes and concerns. You don't want them to become depressed, too.

If you're living with a depressed child, aging parent, or other relative, it also means spending regular time together with your spouse, reconnecting and reaffirming the positive power of your relationship. It's too easy for parents to become so caught up in caring for and talking about a depressed child that they forget to strengthen their own relationship, to enjoy each other's company and support. If you don't reach out to one another, you'll find yourself hugging the empty air of loneliness.

The power of laughter

If one parent is depressed, the other parent often feels guilty having fun. But healthy laughter is probably the best medicine for you at that time. If you have children, they need to spend some time alone with you, the nondepressed parent, to bolster them up, to give them a sense of security and of support. They need to feel good about themselves, to be reassured that it isn't their fault that their other parent is depressed and that you, the nondepressed parent, are in control, even if sometimes you really aren't sure.

"I hadn't realized how depressed my son and I had become living with my husband's depression," a friend said, "until I took my son to the pediatrician for his precollege check up. We sat there, passive and secretly relieved to be out of the house, when a woman walked in with two identical twin boys about nine months old. They were adorable. We couldn't help smiling. Then a couple came in with their fifteen-month-old little girl. She looked at the two little boys, sitting like the proverbial peas in a pod on the floor in their car seats. She looked at one face, then another. Then back to the other. The expression on her face at seeing two babies that she, a baby still herself, recognized as identical, was priceless. We all laughed. It felt so good. My son and I couldn't stop laughing and watching that little girl stare at those babies and how they stared back. We hated to hear the nurse call his name so he had to leave.''

Give yourself that time to ''wallow in joy,'' as one woman called it. ''I find laughter and happiness and wallow in it like a pig back on my daddy's farm,'' she said. ''Then, when I go back home to my poor little girl who is starving herself to death in front of my eyes, I still have some scent of happiness on me.''

Continue your life as usual

As much as possible, continue with your usual activities, your regular exercise, and your regular work schedule. That's difficult to do, much easier to suggest. But it's important to try.

When a loved one becomes depressed your world seems to grow smaller, as though you are looking through the wrong end of a telescope. You begin to cut out social engagements because you hate to leave your family member alone, or you're afraid to, and it's too exhausting to try to tempt him or her into joining you. Before you know it, friends stop calling you. You miss work, letting assignments pile up as your days overflow with caregiving duties. You cancel out on movies and dinner dates, postpone vacations, and then wonder why you feel trapped and depressed yourself.

''My wife and I had planned a family trip for years,'' a stranger on a plane confided to me. ''It was to take our three kids to New York, to see some Broadway shows, take some typically tourist tours, and have dinner at some fancy restaurant. It was going to be our twenty-fifth wedding anniversary to ourselves.

''Then, two years before the big day, Todd, our middle child, became depressed. We never knew what caused it. He just sat like a lump, quit going to high school even though it was his senior year and he would have been the big football star. He withdrew from all his friends. We tried to get him to go for counseling, but he wouldn't.

"It tore my wife and me up. We spent so much time trying to get him well that we didn't have much time left for the other two kids, let alone ourselves. The kids drifted off, had friends we didn't even know, and eventually got into a drinking and drug-using crowd. My only daughter, our youngest, got pregnant and married some salesman from another state. We hardly ever see her or the baby. The oldest boy is okay now but still holds a grudge for the lost years we spent trying to get Todd to be happy again. Both kids resent the fact that because of Todd we never had our dream trip. I wish we had taken it. I wish my wife and I had been able to talk to each other more instead of accusing each other for being to blame for Todd's problem. *He* got depressed, and it destroyed us as a family. I wish I had known what to do."

This man's story was just one of many I heard from total strangers and acquaintances alike. The reactions were typically the same. "You're writing a book about depression? Boy, could *I* have used that a few years ago. . . ." A common theme in many of their stories was regret at having postponed or abandoned dreams and plans. "I was so immersed in the present that I forgot I had a future," said one. "I wish we hadn't let his depression immobilize us as well."

As actor Robin Williams said in the movie *Dead Poets' Society*, "Seize the day!"

Let laughter into your life

Years ago I saw a play on Broadway called *Enter Laughing*. I don't remember anything about the play other than that I know I liked it. I still remember the title, however, because I liked the picture it conjured up. My interpretation was that whatever you've left behind and whatever you're walking into, it's all got to be better if you "enter laughing." I've tried to incorporate that into my life. Try it. It helps.

You may feel you have nothing to laugh about. You

love someone who is depressed. Your life has changed. You feel as though there is nothing and no one you can depend upon. You feel exhausted, cheated, and frazzled. Laugh? Now?

Yes, laugh. It's good for you, physically as well as emotionally. Laughing exercises your muscles, makes you breathe deeply, which forces more oxygen into your lungs and releases chemicals called "endorphins" into your bloodstream. These make you feel relaxed and more at peace with the world. Many studies show that laughter actually can help your immune system, keeping you healthier at a time when you need to be healthy to fight off infection and other illness and lowering your susceptibility to depression. Another benefit of laughter is that it makes you look happier, so people respond to you more positively, just as they tend to retreat from sad, unhappy-looking people.

Never feel that laughter is inappropriate when you're living with a depressed person. Research shows that it actually is healing. It makes you *feel* better, too, and when you feel better about yourself and about life in general, you become less susceptible to the depression within your environment.

Bolster your happiness potential

Happiness truly is a state of mind. It comes from within yourself; thinking really can make it so. Why not give yourself a gift of happiness? Each day, promise yourself that you'll do your best to banish negative thoughts, all worry about things not within your control to change, and guilt. Focus on those things that make you happy. There's a trick involved, you see. As no one can think of two things at once, thinking happy thoughts will prevent your thinking of negative and depressive ones.

Almost ten years ago I was diagnosed with breast cancer. I wasn't shocked by it; the offending lump had felt different from all the others I had experienced in the last twenty years. Somehow I sensed it was malignant this time. I had a biopsy under a local anesthetic. The physician confirmed that, to his surprise, my "cyst" was a malignant tumor. My husband and I went home to weigh my treatment alternatives.

Later that afternoon I felt well enough to go to the neighborhood fish market to buy some fish for dinner. I was wrapped up in my thoughts as I paid the owner and took my fish. "Have a wonderful, beautiful day," he said, as he always did.

My first thought was, "A wonderful, beautiful day? I just found out I've got cancer!" Then I thought a minute, and a big smile forced its way onto my face. He was right. It was a wonderful, beautiful day. I was still around to enjoy it; I had five great kids and a wonderful husband. How lucky I was to be alive.

I've thought about that day often. That comment crowded out any negative thoughts I had carried around since receiving the diagnosis. I couldn't be depressed because my mind was filled with thoughts of wonderful, beautiful things. That doesn't mean, of course, that I never was depressed. I cried in my husband's arms many times; I cried alone, too. I was afraid and angry. I had *written* about breast cancer; I wasn't supposed to have it.

But when I felt blue I did think about the man at the fish store and what he had said. It made me smile then; it still does. Six months ago—far too long to have waited—I went back and thanked him for cheering me up on that scary day.

If you're trying to achieve your maximum happiness potential, it might be helpful to adopt the following suggestions:

- Believe that you deserve to be happy.
- Surround yourself with happy people; happiness is contagious, too.

- Write down three things that make you happy; focus on one of them when you feel depression coming on.
- Allow your guilt to fly away; your loved one's depression is not your fault; you cannot accept blame for it.
- Forgive your loved one for being depressed; he or she cannot help it.
- Give yourself the gift of time; recharge and soothe your spirit through exercise, meditation, listening to music, or whatever gives you pleasure.
- Remember to smile; it not only makes *you* feel happier, but it also makes people smile back.

Practice these suggestions each day so they begin to become habitual. They will help you to be happier and help you to resist catching your loved one's depression.

6

Breaking Communication Barriers

Most of us probably define "communication" as the act of speaking. But just forming recognizable words has as little to do with communication as the ability to walk has to do with running a marathon. It's a beginning, nothing more.

There's more to communication than words

True communication involves far more than just talking. It is a process and involves interaction between the speaker and the listener. When one of these partners suffers from depression, communication may suffer as well. It's hard to talk to someone who is depressed. You often get little reaction. Sometimes you aren't sure if the depressed person even hears you. It's also often difficult to understand what he or she is saying. You may comprehend the words, but their meaning may be somewhat obscured.

"My husband, Frank, keeps saying he's fine," Audrey, a fifty-five-year-old homemaker, said, "but I sense that he isn't, not from anything he says specifically, but from a combination of everything he keeps mentioning and by the defeated way in which he says it. He pretends he's kidding, but he isn't. He complains, for example, that no one in the office ever asks his opinion any more, that the 'young turks' seem to be taking over, getting the choice spots on committees and handling the top accounts. Frank talks about taking early retirement, saying that he is 'over the hill' or that he should be 'put out of misery, like an old racehorse.' I should have picked up on his depression sooner, but I've been preoccupied with my father, who has just been diagnosed with ulcerative colitis, and my own medical problems with menopause. Frank never says he is depressed, not in so many words, but I think he is.''

Often someone who is depressed can't find the words to express his or her feelings and may not even recognize them as depression. You need to dig beneath the words and listen for what isn't being said. It's like translating a foreign language or guessing at a tough game of charades. It's hard work.

It takes two to communicate

Although it may seem easier at times just to ignore someone who's depressed or to deny the fact that he or she is depressed and try to carry on as usual, you do need to learn how to carry on a two-way conversation with someone who is depressed; your own well-being and their life may depend upon it.

In an ideal conversation the listener has the responsibility to pay attention to the speaker, offer eye contact, and give proper feedback through verbal or nonverbal means that the message is being received. It may be as little as occasionally saying ''I see'' or nodding to show understanding or as much as paraphrasing by saying, ''Do you mean that you really don't want to go?'' or ''I hear that you're angry, but I'm still not sure why. Could you explain . . .''

The speaker must keep checking and watching nonverbal cues to be certain that the listener is receiving the same message he or she is sending. This two-way process of conversation is often a difficult one under normal circumstances. When you're trying to reach out to communicate with someone who is depressed, it's even more so. His or her lack of self-esteem may interfere.

If you're in a hurry, for instance, you may reveal that through body language. Most people will sense that you're pressed for time and compress their message to you. A depressed person, on the other hand, may translate that same body language to mean that you don't think what he or she is saying is very important. They'll assume *that* is why you're impatient.

You may say, "You look nice today," meaning it as a compliment, and your depressed relative, whose self-esteem has plummeted, translates it to mean, "You look nice today, but usually you look awful." This "interference" with your communication interchange can be extremely frustrating. It puts you on constant guard and begins to make you a little self-conscious about what you're saying and how you're saying it. Sometimes you feel as though you've gotten caught up in an old Abbott and Costello routine, but this one isn't too funny.

I once found myself trying to cheer up someone who was depressed and engaged in this no-win conversation. Perhaps it sounds vaguely familiar to you, too:

Me: It's a beautiful day today, isn't it?
Depressed Person: It'll rain.
Me: Well, maybe so, but we need the rain. It's been such a dry summer.
DP: Everything's dead. Look at my plants.
Me: Would you like me to water them?
DP: (shrug) What's the use?
Me: (hopefully) It might revive them.
DP: I don't like them anyway.

At this point you may begin to feel a little like Pollyanna or as though you'd like to bang your head against the wall. You may feel like laughing—or crying. Instead, try smiling and changing the subject. Don't expect the reaction to be too different, though. You might as well accept the fact that *you*, well meaning as you are, will not cheer up a depressed person even through wit and sparkling conversation.

What you might consider doing instead is to address the problem head on and say, "You sound so down today. Are you depressed?"

You may only get a shrug or perhaps a denial, but at least you've opened the conversation to reality. It might be just the prompt needed for the person to answer, "I just can't seem to get over Danny's death," or "I never thought I'd miss not going to work. I really do."

Remember that experts stress that if a depressed person sounds in any way as though he or she is considering suicide, you should ask directly if he or she is thinking about killing him- or herself. You will *not* be putting ideas in the person's head, and the depressive may be relieved to know that you understand and will interact to help prevent him or her from self-destruction.

Make time for communication

We all lead busy lives and often can't give undivided attention when someone is speaking, especially when they are as slow and hesitant as depressed people usually are. We become impatient for them to get to the point. And they don't because often they cannot.

It takes time to check for reactions and to solicit or offer feedback, too. At first we feel somewhat silly about doing so. New habits always feels strange at first, and making time to communicate is just that. It's even more awkward when we're trying to talk to someone we care for who is depressed. We hardly can be objective. Emotions keep getting in the way. It hurts us and makes us angry that they don't seem to listen, that they won't tell us what's bothering them. "If you really loved me, you'd tell me," becomes our unreasonable refrain. It's unreasonable because they really don't know what's wrong, and the depression is blocking their ability to tell us even if they *did* know.

What's more, it's difficult to have a two-way exchange when one of the parties (the person who's depressed) offers little eye contact, shows little expression, and shows through body language that he or she is withdrawing from contact with others. Whereas one who is agitated and in a manic state may invade our space, almost sticking his or her face in ours, and chatter constantly, sometimes making little sense, the typically depressed person pulls away, shrinking from any hint of physical or social contact.

How can we continue to try to communicate with our depressed loved ones so that they have the best chance of hearing and understanding what we are saying and, at the same time, reduce our own frustration level? The following suggestions have been offered by numerous family members who have been faced with this problem:

Observe and remain aware of your own body language

When you're trying to communicate with someone who is depressed, you must remain aware of your own body language. Experts claim that 65 to 85 percent of all communication is nonverbal. What we say is often drowned out by our facial expression, body language, and other nonverbal clues. Check to make sure your nonverbal message isn't confusing the one you're giving verbally, such as saying "Take your time, Mother. There's no hurry," while you're frowning, tapping your toe, and sneaking rather obvious looks at your wristwatch.

Don't invade their space.

Be sure there is a comfortable distance between you both so they don't feel threatened. If you've ever tried to have a conversation with someone who keeps moving toward you, almost rubbing noses with you, you know how uncomfortable it makes you. I almost backed into a punch bowl once, doing the backstep constantly to get away from someone like that.

Don't tower above them

It may appear threatening to someone who is depressed or make them feel as though they are in a subservient (lower) position. If they're seated, sit down alongside of them or squat down so you're eye-to-eye.

Maintain eye contact

Don't look around the room, shuffle papers, or pick at your nails as you wait for them to answer. Depressed people have slowed-down reaction times. Often it is difficult for them to process what you have said, formulate their own thoughts, and speak them. Be patient.

Be aware of your own expression

Have you copied their sad expression (easy to do), or is your face relaxed, with a pleasant smile or interested look?

Never underestimate the importance of touch

Unfortunately people often tend to withdraw from those who are depressed rather than moving closer to give them a hug. Yet the physical contact is vitally important, a most-needed nurturing ingredient for all human beings from birth throughout the aging process. Norman Cousins, writing about his own physical illness in his bestselling book *Anatomy of an Illness*, said, "A warm smile and an outstretched hand were valued even above the offerings of modern science, but the latter were far more accessible than the former."[1]

So don't forget to reach out and pat your loved one's hand, put your arm around his or her shoulder, and communicate your love and caring through the extraordinary power of touch.

You may feel that you need a loving touch as well. Communicate that fact to your family, that what you need

most right now is just to be held a little. A hug can be
an important source of comfort and a great stress re-
ducer. I often will say to my husband or one of the kids,
"I need a little hugging time." They all are quick to
respond. I don't feel that it lessens either the act or the
benefit from it because I have to ask for it, either. My
husband and kids are great, but they're not mind readers.

I consider that the benefits of tactile stimulation are so
important—both for the person who is depressed as well
as family members who are fighting to keep from following suit—that I have devoted an entire chapter (Chapter
7) to its discussion.

Learn to Listen

It's amazing how much you can learn by keeping your
mouth shut and perfecting the art of being a good listener. Don't be afraid of silence. It has a language of its
own.

When my brother was hospitalized with the cancer that
would all-too-quickly end his life, I visited often, spending much of my time silently rubbing lotion on his hands
and feet. Our eyes would meet and we'd smile. I'd go
back to rubbing gently, and he would shut his eyes.

One day he said, "Why is it so relaxing when you
visit? We hardly talk."

I thought for a moment, and replied, "I guess we don't
need to."

While we found comfort in the quiet, many people feel
uneasy with silence. They find it difficult to sit in a room
with someone without talking, especially when that person is depressed. But silence shared *is* a form of sharing
and can give comfort to the depressed person who may
find talking tiring and listening to it even more exhausting.

When faced with silence, many of us tend to start chat-
tering about whatever pops into our head, just to make
conversation. But that can be overload to a depressed

person and probably will make him or her react by tuning us out altogether.

I learned to make good use of silence many years ago when I began to interview people for articles. Rather than filling a lull in the conversation by quickly asking the next question on my list, I would often just sit quietly, maintaining eye contact with my interviewee, and waiting. Often the best material came when *they* felt they had to fill the emptiness by speaking.

You can accomplish the same end with patience when you're dealing with someone who is depressed. Don't be afraid to wait them out. They may suddenly speak up to fill the void with some most telling remark.

"I wish I were dead," said one middle-aged man who had been in a depression for many months. When his son Greg began to question him gently he discovered, to his horror, that his father not only wished for death, but had quietly been planning to shoot himself; had actually purchased the gun and knew the day and hour he planned to carry out the act. Fortunately his family was able to get him proper professional treatment in time to forestall such an unhappy event.

Studies of adolescents who have attempted suicide reveal that many of these young people suffered from a sense of isolation and hopelessness, and that their suicide attempt was more of an attempt to express their frustration, anger, and helplessness than to actually kill themselves. Perhaps if their coping and communication skills had been stronger they would have been able to speak out in a healthier way.

In their book *Born to Win*, Muriel James and Dorothy Jongeward said, "Listening is one of the finest strokes one person can give another. Active listening, sometimes called reflective listening, involves verbal feedback of the content of what was said or done along with a guess at the feeling underneath the spoken words or act. . . . Real listening does not necessarily mean agreement."[2]

What better gift to give someone who is depressed than

to let the person know that you care enough about him or her and what he or she is trying to say, to listen? These depressive's self-esteem has been damaged, they feel unworthy, their life seems hopeless, but someone (you) is listening to them, and perhaps that singular act will be a lifeline to which they can cling.

Offer feedback

People who are depressed suffer from poor self-images. They feel inadequate and insecure. Let them know you are listening and that you value what they are saying by offering feedback from time to time. Use comments like, "You're saying that you feel tired today. Does that mean you don't want to get dressed?" or "I hear you saying that nobody cares about you. Do you think I care? . . . What about John? . . ."

Speak slowly

If you've ever been in a foreign country where you only had a rudimentary knowledge of their language, you know how hard it was to understand what they were saying. Even if they understood *you* when you haltingly asked a question, you might have been totally in the dark when they answered it. Although you may have known most of the words spoken, when the natives uttered them they did so too quickly for you to follow. Eventually you just gave up trying. It's often the same experience for someone who is depressed.

Make an effort to speak more slowly and distinctly to the depressed person. Try not to speak while you have a mouth full of food or are chewing gum. If you speak too quickly, as most of us do, it becomes difficult for the depressive to process everything you're saying. It all tends to blur together. From your rapid speech pattern, they also may feel as though they are being rushed, which can be overwhelming. Don't overdo it, however, and sound like an old phonograph record that's winding down. They may lose interest entirely in what you are saying. Be conversational, but slow down your pace.

Never talk down

Never talk to depressed people as though they were children. You will only shatter what little self-esteem they may have left. They are adults and should be treated with respect and dignity. Refrain from sarcasm, too. Attempts at humor may fail because most depressed people don't find humor in anything. Nothing seems funny or joyous to them.

Hold family meetings

Every family communicates differently and in a highly unique fashion. In some families problems are served up at the dinner table along with corn on the cob and fried chicken. In others everyone keeps up the pretense that everything is just fine and that there are no problems whatsoever, despite the fact that everyone really knows that Uncle Joe is depressed and an alcoholic, Susie is unwed and pregnant, and Joey has flunked out of yet another school.

While there really is no single right way of doing things, and every family must work out its special way of communicating, it is important to remember that depression in one member of a family becomes a family issue because of its highly contagious condition.

Many families will try to keep secret the fact that one of their members is depressed. They feel shame that there is a blight on their family's record, that others will think their family is less than perfect. Actually there probably are no perfect families. It relieves a great deal of stress if you accept that at the beginning. Most of us have a few "strange" relatives, a few characters, and a few with problems we'd rather not discuss. But by keeping silent, especially when the problem is one of depression, we isolate ourselves and other family members from outsiders—

friends, professional helpers, and others—who may be able to help, support, or just be of comfort to us.

We all need to talk about our problems. That's why so many of us unburden ourselves to complete strangers on airplanes. It seems safe. The stranger doesn't know us and therefore won't be disappointed to learn that our family has problems. He or she won't be judgmental. We talk to strangers because they're just that, strangers, and we feel we won't ever see them again.

Conversely we don't talk to those we love most. Parents don't tell the kids that they're upset because Grandpa is so depressed. They don't want to make the kids feel badly about Grandpa. But the kids wouldn't. They'd feel sad that Grandpa was depressed, but they'd feel a great deal better knowing what was really wrong with him. They had thought he was angry with them. (Kids tend to personalize things.) Instead of feeling shut out, they'd feel like part of the family.

Family meetings clear the air. They offer time for people to ask questions, come up with ideas for handling problems, and share information and laughter. They make the family feel stronger as a unit, more able to cope, and less vulnerable to depression. (More details on how to set up a family meeting in chapter 10.)

Call for help

People who are depressed usually feel lonely, but this sense of isolation is not theirs alone. Family members also often pull away from friends, partly due to their own growing depression and partly because of a sense of embarrassment or shame in having someone in the family who is suffering from a mental illness.

But this is the time when it's most important for you to speak up, to reach out to your friends and other family members and ask them for help. Don't let pride stand in your way.

Don't expect others to read your mind either. Most people have not perfected the art of ESP. When friends

say, "If there's anything I can do to help," speak up.
Unfortunately they cannot make your loved one happy
again, but they can "babysit" so you can get out of the
house without worrying, or go to the grocery for you, or
perform a myriad of other helpful tasks. Most people
want to help, but they don't know what to do. Use your
family meetings as a time-out period to analyze which
areas you need most help with, then ask for it.

Practice positive self-talk

If you really tune in to what your depressed family
member is saying, you'll realize that much of it is probably quite negative, things such as "I never do anything
right," "I'm just so stupid. I don't know why you put
up with me," "I'm just no good," and so on. It's hard
to know which comes first, the person's self-esteem becoming shaky so they start to tear themselves down or
the loss of self-confidence *because* they continue to be
so negative.

What you may not realize is that you can unconsciously begin to pattern your speech in the same way.
"Man," said the 18th-century German poet and play-
wright Johann Christoph Friedrich von Schiller, "is an
imitative creature." And people are. That's how babies
learn to speak—by imitation. That's also why the daughter of a friend of mine, a native-born Floridian who had
spent little time outside her home state, went to school
in Texas and returned with a Texas accent.

Years ago, when my three sons were small, we took
them all to a basketball game at our local university. We
walked down the aisle in single file, my husband first,
followed by each boy, oldest to youngest. I brought up
the rear. It was worth being the caboose just for the scene
ahead. I saw my husband walking as he usually does,
Marine Corps gait, hands in pockets. Behind him, like
baby ducks in a row, trotted our three boys, also at Marine Corps gait with hands in their pockets. I laughed at
their unconscious imitation and then grew thoughtful at

the powerful message it gave: Our kids imitate us in many ways we never think about.

We also imitate others in the family, both physically and verbally. I have picked up slang terms my kids use; they have picked up expressions of ours. Every so often I catch myself saying something that my mother used to say that I *swore* I'd never say. My friends confess the same horrors.

"I used to hate it when my mother would say, 'Oh, go ahead and do it. I don't care what you do,' " one friend told me. "It usually came after I had been badgering her relentlessly to let me do something, but when she gave up in exhaustion and said that, I usually thought, 'Oh, please. *Do* care.' It really was a no-win situation for her. I swore I'd never say that to my kids, but I do."

When someone you care for tells you through his or her depression that "life is dreary and then we die," boost yourself with positive self talk; remind yourself of all the good things in your life that make it special. Talk to yourself as you would to a good friend whom you were trying to keep in good spirits.

We all need to be comforted, and talking, even to ourselves (which experts refer to as "self-verbalizing") can be most calming. You've seen how babies and toddlers stop fussing when their mother croons to them. It's not what she's saying but rather the sound of her voice. The mantra used in relaxation techniques (see Chapter 10) is much the same. It fills our mind with the same sound that is soothing because it is familiar. Also, because our mind is filled with that sound, we can't think other more distressing thoughts.

So be good to yourself. Choose positive words that make you feel good about yourself and your life. Contrary to that old childhood saying, words *can* hurt you. So select those that have the meaning to make you feel upbeat and happy and discard the others you may have been using. Shakespeare knew the power of words when he wrote, "There is nothing either good or bad, but thinking makes it so.'' Our positive thought messages do affect our sense of well-being. It's another way to inoc- ulate yourself against depression.

At first you may feel a little silly giving yourself happy messages in your mind. As with any new habit, it takes awhile before it becomes routine. So practice.

Become aware of your feelings

Without becoming too self-conscious of your speech, do try to become more aware of its negative content, especially that which may belittle or devalue another family member's sense of self-esteem. It's easy to make one member of the family the scapegoat, attributing ev- erything that goes wrong to that person. Your feelings often are reflected in both your choice of words and your tone of voice, so get in touch with your emotions so you're aware of what you really are feeling. You may be surprised.

Sometimes you really don't want to face what you're feeling. You can't put it into words because saying it aloud makes you feel disloyal and guilty. But keeping anger, resentment, frustration, and other emotions— normal emotions—bottled up inside will hurt you even- tually, creating additional stress, triggering physical illnesses and depression.

That's not to say you should start screaming at those who frustrate you or really tell off your boss or spouse. Instead try speaking out in a different way. If you are artistic, get a canvas or sketch pad and speak through your fingertips. If you're more verbal than artistic, keep a personal journal. Write down your thoughts either in prose or poetry.

''When I was depressed,'' Marty, a forty-year-old re- porter said, ''my psychologist had me write poetry about what I was feeling. I've never written poetry before, so I felt a little self-conscious at first. But it was fun, and it was a wonderful release. Looking through my notebook now, I see how the content changed from expressions of

anger and resentment to one of thankfulness and awareness. The later poems ended on a happy note, along with
my need for more therapy. I still, at times, try to express
my feelings in poetry. It helps. It really does.''

If writing's not your thing, compose a tune, even if
you only pick it out on the piano with just your right
hand. (See, those piano lessons your mother made you
take may pay off after all.) If you're more of a physical
person, shut yourself inside your bedroom and dance.

The important thing is to express yourself in some way,
to assert yourself, which is a way of protecting yourself
from catching your loved one's depression by saying, ''I
have value. My feelings are important. This is how I
feel.''

Improve your communication skills

If more people knew how to communicate—to speak
honestly without accusations, to listen properly and to
give feedback—there might be more lasting marriages,
more successful businesses, more happier people, and
fewer depressed ones. Communication is one of life's
most important skills, yet it is one that receives little
attention in most schools. We teach children how to spell
and to punctuate what they have written but not to make
sure they have selected the specific words to express the
exact meaning of what they're trying to say. Few schools
offer courses in public speaking or private communication. At a time when they are so vulnerable to emerging
emotions, our adolescents are often rendered speechless.

There are ways, however, to improve communication
skills regardless of one's age. Many schools, universi-
ties, religious institutions, and civic groups offer semi-
nars and courses in assertiveness training, public
speaking, and effective communication skills. In addition, many psychologists, social workers, and other mental health professionals have been trained to help
individuals and entire families to learn how to communicate more effectively both personally and in a family

setting. Even if your depressed family member won't contribute or even refuses to attend group sessions, the rest of the family can gain important knowledge and experience under the watchful tutelage of an objective professional.

As with many skills, communication skills are learned and can be improved with practice. You may have picked up poor communication habits as a child that are still ill-serving you. Strive for improvement. As with other life skills, the art of communication gets better with practice. Effective communication is probably one of the best stress reducers I know and, fortunately, it's habit-forming and can even be contagious.

Endnotes

1. Norman Cousins, *Anatomy of an Illness* (New York: Bantam Books, 1981).
2. Muriel James and Dorothy Jongeward, *Born to Win*, (Reading, Addison-Wesley Publishing Co., 1971).

7

Learn the Importance
of Touching

This chapter reflects my bias. I'm a "toucher." So's my husband. After thirty years of marriage, he still reaches out to grab my hand when we cross a street; sensitive to my flying fears, he takes my hand at takeoffs and landings. Occasionally he'll absentmindedly give my fanny a pat in public. We still hug, and caress our kids even though they're all now legally adults.

But our Puritanical society is not known for touching. Friends may look as though they're kissing, but actually they usually just smack the air or occasionally brush against a cheek. Sports offer the only "approved safe touching" between men; hugging and slaps on the behind are condoned on the playing field and in the locker room. We warn our kids (rightfully so) about "bad touching," but forget to encourage "good touching" by our actions.

You may have been raised in a family in which no one touched each other openly, in which fathers shook hands with sons and hugs were hoarded. The only acceptable public touching was with the family's dog or cat.

"I was fifty years old before my mother ever hugged me," a woman confessed to me over lunch. "I never knew what made her finally do it." She seemed surprised when I wondered aloud if she had asked her mother why.

"Oh, no. We never talked about things like that," she answered.

On the other hand, you may have enjoyed a family in which all members felt comfortable expressing their love and encouragement through caresses, pats, hugs, and kisses.

The power of this "laying on of hands" is hardly a new concept. Recorded from earliest time on the walls of caves, our language is still filled with expressions that attest to the importance of touch, such as "Lend a helping hand," "Reach out," "Just the right touch," and "That's touching." Physicians, nurses, and clergy alike know well the therapeutic benefits—both physical and psychological—that come from touching a patient or troubled soul.

Doctors have discovered that premature babies housed in sterile bassinets actually gain weight faster when they are tactilely stimulated. Many hospitals now have programs featuring volunteers who rock and cuddle babies who, for various reasons, have failed to thrive. Geriatric studies reveal positive effects when nursing-home staffs are encouraged to pat a shoulder, hold a hand, or gently squeeze a patient's arm.

Sherry Suib Cohen, co-author of *The Magic of Touch*, has this to say about touching: "You can't give a touch without getting one right back. You can talk, listen, smell, see, and taste alone, but touch is a reciprocal act."[1]

Touch is so valuable to most people's well-being that to restrict it becomes a powerful force. In India about a fifth of the population is considered to be such outcasts that these people are referred to as "untouchables." People who suffer from depression often feel as lowly and unworthy, and pull away from those who most want to reach out and speak through the language of touch. Ironically, by their actions, the depressed keep us at arm's length, preventing our touches which might have reassured them that they are valued, are wanted, are loved.

How to "reach out" to a depressed person

We, who love someone who is depressed, find ourselves in a quandary. If we disregard the feelings of the depressed person and reach out to them anyway, we might break through their resolve and give comfort. Yet, on the other hand, it is possible that the depressed would see these actions as confirmation of the fact that their wishes are unimportant, that *they* are unimportant, and that no one listens to what they have to say, so why bother?

Nevertheless, knowing that those who are depressed need the reassurance and comfort of touch, most of us keep trying to soothe our agonized loved ones. It sounds easy enough: A family member is depressed, so everyone should make more of an effort to hug or kiss him or her. But it doesn't work that way. The person who is depressed feels unworthy of so much attention. Instead of responding positively, the sufferer pulls away in added isolation.

How does that make us feel? We feel hurt, rebuffed, rejected. What do we do? If we're like most people, we eventually give up and say, "To heck with you. I tried." Feeling self-conscious and frustrated, we pull back or walk away. The depressed person sees this as *our* rejection of them, which only proves that they really were unworthy after all.

So what can you do? It's difficult to keep reaching out to someone who doesn't respond or worse who pulls away from your touch as though your hand were a hot poker. But you must keep trying, much as you try to comfort and cuddle an over-tired toddler who screams and tries to pull away through frustration and fatigue. Remind yourself that it's the depression that's causing your loved one to pull away, that *you* are not being rejected. It's your caring and love—the things that the depressed person wants (and needs) so desperately but cannot accept that he or she deserves—that is being rejected. You must be persistent but not overwhelming.

You can acknowledge the depressed person's rejection of your attempts and at the same time let him or her know that you are still there and that you will keep reaching out until you both connect. Stress the fact that you are patient and willing to wait but that you will keep trying while you wait. Don't expect an answer or reaction. It may take a few tries before the person can accept a hug or even a gentle touch. Also, don't be surprised if, once he or she does, it releases a torrent of tears.

Let massage work for you

Massage is a specialized form of touching that can help to keep your spirits up during this difficult period and may even benefit someone who is depressed if you can talk him or her into trying it. Despite what you may read in some of the popular magazines, massage is scarcely a new technique for stress reduction and improving mood. It was used by the ancient Greeks and Romans as well as by many Far Eastern cultures for centuries for both its relaxation and therapeutic benefits.

I discovered massage about ten years ago while on vacation. It was about the only activity available at a particular resort that didn't require physical exertion, and I felt too keyed up to read or sleep. By the time the allotted one hour was up, I felt innervated and ready to move mountains. (Some people feel relaxed and ready to sleep. It's a very personal reaction.) When I returned to the real world, I reorganized my hectic schedule to make time for a reasonably regular massage.

The massage therapist (if male called *masseur*; if female, *masseuse*) comes to my home with her specially constructed massage table. I unplug the phone, turn off the air-conditioning, and dim the lights. She begins with my neck (a major tension spot for me) and ends an hour later working on my back.

There are various types of massage, although all involve pressure, kneading, or stroking. Swedish massage, probably the best known, incorporates quick strokes into the bodywork, while sports massage, which I prefer, has the therapist going deep into the muscles, improving circulation and offering a therapeutic benefit. It also improves the mobility of the joints. Shiatsu is a Japanese form of body therapy in which the therapist uses finger pressure to release blocked energy. With all these forms of massage, the amount of pressure varies depending on the therapist and your personal preference. You need to experiment and then communicate your requirements to your massage therapist.

People also differ in their desire for background music or silence. If your massage is in a spa, "Y," or beauty shop, you may have some distractions from background noises. I prefer total silence so I can experience almost a floating sensation while I allow my mind to go blank. I once suffered through an hour-long massage with a masseuse who couldn't stop talking. It not only wasn't relaxing, it also made me tense with frustration for being wishy-washy and not having the confidence to tell her to please be quiet. Be assertive. You're paying for the massage.

ALWAYS check references, especially if the therapist is coming to your home. Many states require these professionals to be licensed. Contact your state's department of professional regulation to see if it requires such licensing. If so, ask the massage therapist for his or her credentials.

Recently an adaptive form of massage has come to industry. Massage therapists come to people's office or work place and have the clients straddle a special massage chair with their face resting on a cushioned pillow with a cut-out breathing space. The therapist then works out kinks and tension in the neck, back, and arms, the most common spots for stress to rest.

Does it work? Ask anyone who has ever had a backrub. Even my father in a nursing home, who responds to very little else, responds positively to having his neck or forehead rubbed. He smiles and looks like he is about to purr.

Massage doesn't even have to be done by a human hand. Have you ever had a cat sit on your stomach purring and kneading? I have and find it a most relaxing and pleasurable experience. A dog's licking your hand or face also can be a form of massage, though a somewhat slobbery one. There are massage machines as well that serve to work out the kinks, although they cannot duplicate the wonders of a human (or animal) touch.

Researchers, not content with the layperson's response that "massage makes me feel good," have studied the scientifically measurable effects of massage. They have found that the stimulation effect of the therapist's hands on a person's body along with the heat sensation created by the rubbing or stroking can help to increase the circulation of blood flowing into tissues, restoring them to a more healthful condition. Other studies reveal that older people with pets to stroke (and to receive attention from in return) tend to have lowered blood pressures and be less depressed. Massage therapist Ava Englund verified that by saying, "Psychologists often have asked me to work on their chronically depressed clients."

I have experienced the same positive effects of massage when I have been feeling just a little blue. Smudge, my fifteen-year-old cat, seems to sense when my mood is low. He'll climb out of the wire file basket that he's managed to curl up in, or wiggle his way out of the brown grocery bag that he's confiscated on the floor, and jump up into my lap. He'll lick my hand with his warm, rough tongue, just as I've seen adult animals lick their young. His touch is so intense, so soothing, that the corners of my mouth soon begin to crinkle. I chuckle and stroke him back. My feline massage therapist has made me laugh again.

I must hasten to say that I'm not suggesting that you run out to your local Humane Society to buy a kitten or a puppy for the depressed person in your family. While it might help—and I've heard people describe personal situations in which the addition of a new pet did ease someone's depression—the added responsibility could be overwhelming, too.

Although some people really do not like to be touched— usually due to upbringing or a bad experience—most of us seem to get relief from massage. If you're dealing with the tensions that come with having someone in your family who is depressed, try massage. You deserve some comforting, too.

Informal touches

There are other types of touches that feel good and can boost your self-esteem. I call them "informal touches," but they really are strokes that you either give yourself or arrange for others to give. Many of us feel embarrassed to admit that we crave these informal touches. Making a date for a manicure seems frivolous when we have someone at home who is depressed, but it isn't. The enforced time-out as you sit, your hand in someone else's hands, can be important as it recharges you emotionally and physically.

"I used to eat when I felt blue," Kelly Sue, a young consultant, confided. "Then a friend gave me a certificate for a manicure as a 'no-reason' gift. It was great. I loved the way it made me feel. I stopped my compulsive eating. I stopped biting my nails as well. It may sound strange, but having a weekly manicure makes me feel better about myself."

As the skin is our largest organ, there are many areas that give us comfort sensations when they are touched. You need to get in touch (that word again) with your own body to discover what feels good to you.

Some people find that at the beauty or barber shop, when someone rubs their head with soothing warm water and shampoo, is the "mini-massage" that perks them up. It stimulates the scalp and can make you feel more upbeat than before. If your depressed relative will allow you to, make a date for him or her as well, or try a home shampoo and a vigorous hair brushing and see if that bolsters the spirits a little. If nothing else it certainly will help to spruce up a depressed person's appearance, which is an important aspect in improving one's self-image.

There are twenty-six bones in the human foot. Sometimes it feels as though each one is hurting. I've discovered that I can make myself feel peppier on days that I really am exhausted by rubbing lotion onto my aching feet and then massaging the ointment into each toe. Although it's more relaxing when it's done by a massage therapist, it's soothing nevertheless when it's done by your own hand. Try it.

Others swear by facials. I personally don't like them, but those that do say it banishes their own blues and makes them feel more alert and ready to deal with what's on their plate.

Naturally none of these informal touches will alter a serious depression, but they *can* help to make you feel better about yourself and at the same time offer you a few minutes' respite. If you feel deprived of touch—and it's easy to feel that way when your spouse or significant other is depressed—make time to pamper yourself with touch. It's time well spent.

Sex can be a "touchy" issue

You may think it strange to be reading about sex in a book about depression. After all, you read in one of the earlier chapters that one of the signs of depression is a lack of interest in sex. It is. Some drugs prescribed for depression also may inhibit the sex drive. But that doesn't mean that you as the spouse or significant other has lost interest as well. You shouldn't feel guilty about having these desires, either. It's a normal part of life.

For some, however, the depressed spouse's lack of interest in sex seems to be contagious. Sex may be the last

thing on your mind right now. You may be understandably tired from all the extra chores and responsibilities
you now perform while the depressed person is unable
to do them. You may have picked up a little of his or her
depression as well. Although you may have become sexually turned off in response to the depressed person's
attitude toward you and life in general, you may still feel
the need for intimacy and miss the lovemaking of the
pre-depressed days.

If your idea of a solution is to run out and find a lover,
slow down and think again. While that action might tem-
porarily satisfy your need for sexual intercourse and release your sexual tensions, it also would serve to affirm
to the depressed person that he or she truly was so un-
desirable that you had to find somebody else. It also
might create numerous additional problems, including
AIDS or a host of new and not-so-new sexually transmitted diseases, at a time when you already have your
hands full trying to cope with a depressed family member. There *are* other alternatives, so try them instead.

You can get sexual release through masturbation, man-
ually or by using a vibrator, although for many people
religious beliefs or carryover childhood guilt prevents
their utilizing this option. The problem with this solution, however, is that it only satisfies sexual tension
without addressing the need for intimacy.

Sex, if it's mutually "good," satisfies far more crav-
ings than just the need for orgasm. It offers comfort to
the participants as they touch and cuddle each other. You
feel protected, desired, and needed. You enjoy stroking
and touching your partner and being stroked and touched
in return.

Many couples, due to illness or other reasons, have
found that mutual hugging and kissing can be somewhat
satisfying without actually having sexual relations. Your
depressed partner may find surprising enjoyment just lying in your arms, feeling your support and strength much
as a helpless child senses it when being held and rocked

by a loving parent. While you may resent the shift in role from lover to parent figure, focus on the comfort you are giving to your distressed mate—as well as the tactile pleasure you are receiving—and be assured that once the depression has lifted, your former role can once more be resumed.

Now's the time to be honest about your feelings. You may have never been comfortable talking about sexual matters. This becomes a difficult time to begin a dialogue, because a depressed person often finds communication difficult. Try, however, to share your feelings with your spouse, and let him or her know what your needs are.

"We never talked about sex," a fifty-year-old woman confided. "We were the 'weekend warriors,' who just made love on Saturday night and Sunday noon. It seemed to satisfy us both. Since Joe's been depressed, though, we haven't had sexual relations since . . . I really can't remember when. It began to bother me. I felt angry, rejected by him. I've gained a little weight over the years, but I'm still reasonably attractive. I felt frustrated and even fantasized about finding a lover. Finally I said to him one night, 'Look, I know you don't feel like making love right now. I wish you did, but I can accept that you don't. But can't you just hold me a little? I miss it.'

"He looked at me in surprise. I was a little surprised myself. As I said, we never had been that open about things like that. But he reached over and took me in his arms. I can't tell you how great it felt. I felt safe again and so comforted. I think he enjoyed it, too. Reassuring him that we could embrace without it being a prelude to sex took the pressure off, I think. Now we often fall asleep in each other's arms or just holding hands. We still haven't made love, but we still feel in love. I discovered that touching, not sex, was what I had missed."

A number of people with depressed spouses said that the loss of the physical relationship—not just sexual—was one of the most difficult parts of coping with their loved one's depression. Some used massage, gently rubbing or stroking the depressed person's back, neck, arms, and legs with lotion or warmed oil to stay "in touch" through this physical contact. It offered comfort to them as well. Although I was not able to conduct a proper study to determine actual statistics, I would guess that by continuing some semblance of physical contact, these couples would have an easier time restoring post-depression intimacy than would couples who gave up touching for the duration of the depression.

Try to keep from heaping guilt on your depressed loved one if he or she withdraws from physical contact. Chances are the guilt is there already without you adding to it. Being taunted or blamed for a failed sex life will only serve to make the person's self-image worse than it already is and pile another failure onto his or her ever-growing perceived list.

Although many physicians and psychologists feel comfortable talking about sexual issues, there are, unfortunately, many who don't. You may discover, to your surprise and chagrin, that your otherwise caring and knowledgeable professional stammers and stutters when you try to discuss sexual problems and makes it obvious that he or she doesn't like talking about "those things."

I had my gall bladder out when I was thirty, albeit some time ago. The day I was to be released from the hospital, my surgeon came to give me post-op instructions about when I could drive, climb stairs, lift the children, and so on. He asked if I had any questions.

"Just one," I said. "What about sex?"

He actually blushed, mumbled something about how lucky my husband was, and fled, leaving me to make my own decision.

From experiences others have shared with me, this is far from an unusual reaction, even today in our "enlightened" age. If you sense your physician or psychologist isn't comfortable with sexual issues, don't clam up. Find someone who will talk about them, or contact the American Association of Sex Educators, Counselors, and Therapists, a professional organization for experts in that particular field. For the names of certified sex therapists in your state, send a stamped, self-addressed, business-size envelope to:

AASECT
Suite 1717
435 N. Michigan Avenue
Chicago, IL 60611
Phone: (312) 644-0828

Sometimes a couple's physical relationship is strained, not by one of the partner's depression but rather by that of another family member, such as a child or parent living in the same house. It's difficult to feel romantic when your depressed child weeps or tosses restlessly with insomnia in the next room, or you hear your parent opening the bathroom medicine cabinet and wonder if you should get up to check.

Normal caressing and embracing between lovers may become strained with a depressed family member looking on. You may feel somewhat self-conscious or worry that your actions will only make the depressed person feel more isolated or alone. So, without design, you first stop kissing each other good-bye before going to work, then you forgo rubbing your lover's shoulder as you walk by, and before you know it, you suddenly realize that your family member's depression has crept into the bedroom with you and smothered the intimacy that once blossomed there.

If that should happen—or, hopefully, before it does—discuss the problem with your spouse. Problems acknowledged may then be solved. You might plan evenings out during which you can enjoy each other's company over dinner without the all-prevailing depressive atmosphere. Take a weekend off and either go out of town or check into a local hotel or motel and enjoy your privacy. Find activities just the two of you can enjoy, such as tennis, golf, gardening, or sailing.

Don't ever apologize for wanting some time alone with the person you love. It will make you both less vulnerable to the depression that otherwise fills your home and will recharge you for the energies necessary for caring for the depressed person. Promise yourselves, however, that when you are alone together you will refrain from talking constantly about the family member who is depressed. Leave him or her at home in your thoughts as well for the time being and revel in each other's love.

Touch, that most magic entity, has the power to heal, to allow you moments for mending, to regroup the energies so constantly spent when you're dealing with someone who is depressed. If other family members don't sense your need (or you theirs), ask for a hug or some holding time. It never minimizes the effect because you have to ask—and with hugs and holds, the more you give, the more you truly receive.

Endnote

1. Harriet Harvey and Sherry Suib Cohen, *The Magic of Touch*, (New York: Harper & Row, Publishers, Inc., 1987).

8

Fighting Depression Through Relaxation Techniques

This chapter contains a potpourri of relaxation ideas to help you reduce some of the stress you are experiencing and to help prevent you from "coming down" with depression as well. All of these may not appeal to you; hopefully some of them will. They all are proven and have helped others.

The major hurdle you must cross is the feeling that you don't have time for yourself. While I'm not minimizing the fact that you probably have many more burdens than ever before as you try to care for someone who is depressed, I'm also stressing from personal experience, supported by research and testimony from experts, that if you don't take care of yourself FIRST, you will be in no shape to care for others. What's more, by neglecting yourself you will only become more vulnerable to becoming depressed as well.

Unfortunately I cannot list the "Ten Things to Help You Relax." It would make things easier by far. But what relaxes you may make me a nervous wreck. My niece relaxes by jumping out of a perfectly safe airplane—with a parachute, of course. Just the thought of that makes me feel anxious. Each person must determine by trial and error what works best for him or her. But try something. You'll never know how good you can feel if you don't begin looking today.

Progressive relaxation

Babies and toddlers instinctively know how to relax. When they're tired, they fall asleep. It doesn't matter if they're on the floor, on your shoulder, or riding in the stroller. They just get limp and zap, they're sound asleep, breathing deeply in that angelic way we adults so envy.

Most of us have forgotten how to achieve that state of total relaxation. But the good news is that it can be re-learned easily. The technique is called "progressive relaxation." There are many books and tapes that you can buy or get from the library that describe this technique. Unfortunately many of them make the process sound much more complicated than it really is. Some people are turned off by the mystical mumbo jumbo of it all. It's too bad, because progressive relaxation is really a most simple—and valuable—technique.

The purpose of progressive relaxation is to help you relax. The theory is simple: If you're relaxed, you can't be tense. If you're not tense, you feel better. Your blood pressure may lower and your heart rate slow down. You also may strengthen your immune system, which can be undermined through continued stress. Just reading about how to achieve relaxation won't relax you, of course, any more than reading a diet book will make you slim or watching a videotape on golf will put you on tour. You need to learn the fundamentals and then practice, practice, practice.

The theory of relaxation "on cue," so to speak, is nothing new. Religious leaders have used various forms of progressive relaxation for centuries, calling it "meditation," "yoga," or other names. In modern times, however, physiologist Edmund Jacobson became convinced that prolonged tension could trigger certain illnesses. In *Progressive Relaxation: A Physiological and Clinical Investigation of Muscular States and Their Significance in Psychology and Medical Practice*, published in 1938, he explained that by becoming aware of certain areas of muscular tension in their bodies, people could then learn how to reduce that tension. Probably the most popular recent book to discuss the subject of relaxation is *The Relaxation Response*, written by Herbert Benson, M.D with Miriam Z. Klipper.

There are basically two forms of progressive relaxation—active and passive. Both work to achieve a deep relaxation. Discover which you prefer and then practice it until it becomes part of your everyday activities, until you can call on it at will when you feel tension creeping back into your body. It will help relax you and provide a protective shield against the fatigue that makes you susceptible to depression.

Active progressive relaxation

Until you become more comfortable with the fundamentals, practice this technique in private, where you know you won't be disturbed. Once you've mastered it, you can use it at your desk, while you're working at home, or sitting in services at your church or synagogue. The goal, of course, is to be able to achieve deep relaxation in the midst of chaos, not only when you're sitting quietly at home.

Loosen your tie and waistband. Sit in a comfortable chair or lie on the bed or couch. Close your eyes and let your thoughts fly out of your mind. Begin by first tightening, then relaxing, your toes, then your ankles, the calves of your legs, and on up your body to your facial and scalp muscles. Concentrate on the warm, relaxed sensations that come after you release the tension in your muscles.

By doing this you are reeducating yourself to the way both tension and relaxation feels. I discovered this most vividly after returning home to Florida after a hectic two-week trip to New York City, a place I adore, although I do find the noise level, crowds, and other tensions stressful.

I was downtown waiting for a car to pass before crossing the street. Suddenly I became aware that my face felt more relaxed. I quickly did a body stress inventory, checking out my neck and arms—prime tension areas for me—and realized that I did feel more relaxed there as well. I had not been aware of the increased tension level in New York, but now that I was home, the sensations in my face, neck, and arms felt much warmer and more relaxed. Knowing this, I now practice relaxation techniques much more faithfully, especially when I travel. It helps with my nervousness on planes as well.

Passive progressive relaxation

This type of relaxation is very similar to its active counterpart, but you don't tense your muscles first. Instead you talk them into relaxation, focusing first on your toes and saying "My toes are warm. Warm toes. Relaxed. They float. They are relaxed. I am calm." Then you move up to the rest of your body, not forgetting your hands and fingers. Your "mind messages" crowd out any other thoughts as you relax all your muscles. Breathe in and out at a regular pace. Picture some scene that means relaxation to you, or concentrate on a particular word or phrase.

Don't pay a lot of money to get "your special mantra." You really don't need it. Just come up with a word that's special to you—"relax," "peace," "love," "God," "Jesus," "calm," and so on. It also can be simply a sound, like "Ummm" or "Ahhhh." You can't hold two thoughts in your mind at once, so if you concentrate on the relaxation thought, all others are banished. They may pop into your head from time to time, but that's perfectly normal. Just go back to your word or phrase and those other thoughts will move out. Focus on your phrase and how relaxed you are, on the floating sensation as tension disappears from your body, on the peace you feel. Just writing these words makes my face muscles relax. My eyelids feel heavy, my breathing is deep and even.

At first practice this technique at least once a day for ten to twenty minutes. If you can make time for twice a day, it's even better, but experts warn against more than that.

"The idea is not to withdraw from the world," said one, "but to be equipped to handle stressful situations by being able to feel relaxed and release the tension you feel."

Once you've mastered this technique in private, you can incorporate it in your daily activities. After all, that's where you probably will need it most. I practice passive relaxation when I'm driving and waiting for the light to turn green; I use it at times while I'm on the phone; I've used it often while writing this book. When I feel frustrated, depressed, or angry, I turn to the relaxation techniques that have, by now, become almost second nature to me. In fact, when I begin with "My toes feel warm," I can almost feel the rest of my muscles ease up as well.

"I try," you may complain, "but all my problems and 'shoulds' keep popping into my head. How can I free my mind? I'll never relax with all these thoughts making me tense."

It's perfectly natural to have to struggle to clear your mind at first. Just let those thoughts drift by, like bits of seaweed in the surf. When they try to attach themselves to you, concentrate instead on your word or phrase and keep floating along in relaxation. Visualize those problems or extraneous thoughts actually moving away from you as though you were a magnet and had reversed the magnetic field, repelling all stressful thoughts and forming a safe protective barrier around yourself. Float, breathe in and out, and relax.

Be patient. You wouldn't expect to become fluent in a foreign language overnight. You'd struggle with vocabulary and forget how to conjugate the same verbs you learned just the day before. Learning to relax on demand is the same. So practice faithfully, and when you feel stress building up in you, practice until the natural thing is to float into your relaxation mode rather than tensing up.

As you become better at relaxation, you might discover an important side effect—others around you may want to know your secret. Possibly even the person who is depressed will try progressive relaxation and just for a moment be able to find release from tension.

Remind yourself to practice relaxation by putting a mirror over your telephone. When you see yourself frowning, tell your face to grow warm and relax. Stick a note on your computer screen or typewriter, reminding yourself to relax your neck and shoulders, to float for a few minutes. A friend uses blue dot stickers to remind her. They're on her telephone, bathroom mirror, and even on her purse and briefcase.

Conjure up a special view or scene that makes you feel relaxed. As I described in another book, "The scene that is soothing to me is an old-fashioned rope swing hanging from a tree on top of a hill—not a very high hill. It overlooks a bay with sailing ships just on the horizon. I can almost see myself swinging back and forth on that swing and feel the gentle breeze blowing against my face. The smell of salt fills my head. I slowly breathe in and out, thinking "calm," "calm," with every exhalation. I think the motion of the swing reminds me of my childhood, when I had no sense of urgency about anything and could swing for hours watching a butterfly flit around the sandbox or seeing clouds form into shapes like pictures. To me, it's soothing, relaxing, and means peace."[1]

What scene brings that feeling to you? Is it a childhood scene? Your first love? Some accomplishment? Perhaps it's sitting in a rowboat, watching the bobber at the end of your cane fishing-pole line bounce up and down, up and down, like a tireless jumping jack in the water. One woman told me her relaxation scene was to visualize a kite with colorful streamers floating, dipping, and carried aloft in the breeze. As long as she concentrated on the kite she felt calm and relaxed. Another said her scene was the inside of a dark cave. Someone with claustrophobia might feel as though they were suffocating, but for this woman, it represented peace and tranquility. Everyone's different.

Exercise

The passiveness exhibited by someone who is depressed can quickly affix itself to you before you recognize it. You may feel lethargic and find it difficult to get up in the morning. Saturday afternoon may arrive and find you still in your robe and slippers. Making plans for any type of activity or social life may suddenly seem like too much effort.

It's understandable, but it need not be inevitable. You can run away from passiveness—literally. Exercise, whatever form it takes, is important in chasing away fatigue and its ever-present companion, growing depression.

You may think you're too tired to exercise. I often feel that way. But once the inertia is broken and you actually *are* exercising, it is amazing how good it feels and how energetic you feel afterward. It's the getting started that's the tough part of exercise, not the actual act of exercising.

"Okay, okay," you say. "What type of exercise is best?" The best exercise is whichever form you'll do. It doesn't have to be just one type either. You can walk, join an aerobics class, go dancing, or you can just jog.

Many people jump into a specific form of exercise because a friend is doing it, decide they don't like it, and give up on exercise. Better to take a while to consider your choices, determining what *you* enjoy, when you can make time for it, and what you can afford to pay in case it requires a specific wardrobe or equipment.

Take time to think about your individual preference when it comes to exercise. If you do something you like, you're a lot more likely to stay with it. Ask yourself some questions. Do you prefer exercising alone or in a group? In the morning or later in the day? Something you can do spontaneously, like walking or running, or activities usually requiring a reservation and therefore a commitment to show up, like tennis or racquetball?

Don't run out and buy expensive equipment like skis and ski outfits, a tenspeed bicycle, treadmills or stair-climbing machines, until you know for sure that it's a "perfect marriage." All these items are available for rent in most communities. Never assume you'll use athletic equipment just because you paid so much for it. My non-scientific Shimberg Survey tells me that if all the dust-gathering stationary bikes in America were laid end to end, they'd reach from California to Connecticut.

While it's unlikely that your depressed family member will join you in exercise, offer him or her the opportunity. Remember, however, that someone who has anorexia, a serious eating disorder with a depressive component, may jump at the chance to burn up even more calories and may become a compulsive runner.

When are you supposed to find time for exercise with all your added responsibilities? It's tough. There never really is any time for exercise when you're not particularly "into" exercise. You have to make it. There is no one specific time that's right for everyone either. Some people jump out of bed a little earlier; others take their lunch hour to work out at the gym. Those with treadmills (like me) walk before work in front of the television and combine keeping up on world affairs with a fast walk. Still others prefer to walk after work, enjoying the sights and fresh air as they relax from their day's efforts through exercise. Although research continues to support varying conclusions, the theory at this writing is that twenty to thirty minutes of daily walking or running is sufficient for maximum benefits. More than that may cause physical injury.

Exercise offers more than its important physical benefits. It gives you a chance to get away from a depressive environment and to join with friends and acquaintances who feel good about life and about themselves. It offers opportunity for laughter, an element that may be seriously lacking in your life right now. It will help you feel better about yourself, your life, and even may offer you a refreshed perspective when it comes to dealing with that special person in your life who suffers from depression. It isn't running away from your problems—it's running (or walking, biking, and so on) to help you handle your problems.

Massage

This important relaxation technique is discussed in detail in the previous chapter. If you missed it, go back and read it now. Even if you don't like being touched, you may gain a new perspective on the value of massage and of those informal touches that can soothe.

Hobbies

Work, for many of us, is our hobby. While that's good in that it means we enjoy what we do, it's also bad because it means we don't have any outlet to relax us when life becomes too stressful.

Some people consider sports their hobby, but they're often the same ones you see bending their putter in half or throwing their shoe at the television set when their team's quarterback throws yet another interception. Relaxing? Hardly.

Compare that with the fisherman, for whom the act of fishing is relaxing—it really doesn't matter if anything bites or not; or the gardener mucking about in the dirt, talking to the petunias and the pansies; or the cook, painter, needlework enthusiast, bike rider, or music lover. Look at the hobbyist's face if you wonder if hobbies are good for you. Chances are there's a trace of a smile, no wrinkled brow, relaxed lips, and little, if any, tension in the cheek muscles. The person may be intent, but he or she is clearly enjoying the pursuit.

My father used to spend hours sifting through postage stamps, examining each one carefully under a magnifying glass, fingering it gently before he found its exact place in one of his stamp books. He was relaxed with his hobby. In his younger days he did woodwork, crafting book ends, picture frames, and furniture for my dollhouses. Through his example I learned the value of "time out," a period of withdrawing from others and from usual activities, to refuel yourself in some quiet and pleasurable pursuit.

Reading and needlepoint became my hobbies. My nightstand is filled with an eclectic pile of books stacked high and is beginning to resemble Pisa's famed tower. My couch and living-room chairs cannot hold another needlepoint pillow (so I'm working on a fire screen).

If none of these pursuits tempts you, try the unusual. Dr. Stephen Allen, Jr., a medical doctor with a specialty in family medicine and son of entertainer and author Steve Allen, took up juggling to relax him. Former football great Roosevelt Grier and the late performer Mary Martin became needlepoint experts and admitted it was most effective in relieving stress. Take piano lessons or invest in CDs (compact discs, not certificates of deposit) and you'll find both to be investments in relaxation. Even professional athletes in most sports receive a time out period, so give yourself a break. Bake bread, go sailing or shelling, but do find something that's specially yours to pique your interest, to take you away from depression, and to bring a sense of peace to your soul.

Take refuge in water

For most of us, water offers a special attraction. Some may say it's because we spent nine months floating in amniotic fluid in our mother's womb. Others go back further and claim it dates back to when the first sea creature flopped onto the beach and began the evolution into what we are today. I think it's simply because the touch of water on our skin feels good.

When you feel too much tension around you and sense that you may be absorbing some of the depression in your home, try "immersion therapy," a term my friend coined when she took to her tub.

Send the kids to a neighbor or get a sitter if you have little ones; turn on the answering machine or muffle the telephone with a pillow. Fill up the tub with warm water and add bath oil or bubble bath. Don't make the water too hot as it can make you faint.

Climb in, close your eyes, and visualize that favorite spot of yours that makes you feel relaxed. Breathe deeply and savor the scent of the bath oil. Let your feet bob up, let your hair get wet. Relax. Spend half an hour in your personal spa and enjoy it.

If you have access to a hot tub or swimming pool, use them, too. Enjoy the buoyancy as your body bobs up and down in the water. Accept the playfulness that water seems to bring out in us all. Relax.

Daydreams

Daydreams are a type of visualization but often take you off in a relaxed fantasy you never expected. What got you in trouble in English class can actually be good for you now as most experts feel that daydreaming, for many people, is analogous to relaxation and meditation because it tends to relieve tension. Dr. Thomas D. Borkovec, a psychologist at Pennsylvania State University agrees that daydreams can be a pleasant form of temporary relaxation, but warns, "Don't replace one habit (i.e. getting overstressed) with another. Don't get too removed. Daydreaming should never be used as escape, but rather as a brief release and respite."

Think of your daydreaming as the valve on the pressure cooker that wiggles when the steam builds up and lets enough off so the whole thing doesn't blow up. Let your senses—the scent of lilacs, the feel of velvet, the taste of licorice, the sight of autumn leaves at their peak, the sound of children playing—carry you off in your mind to a peaceful place. Relax and enjoy this gift of drift.

Take a nap

As great as America is in many ways, we, as a nation, have never really caught on to the advantages of the siesta. Babies take naps, of course, but toddlers proclaim quite proudly that they are "too big to take a nap." Silly kids. They shouldn't let go of such a good thing.

According to William C. Dement, M.D., Ph.D., director of the Stanford Sleep Disorders Clinic and Research Center, "Current public consensus appears to hold that napping represents a sign of weakness. However, if our schedules absolutely keep us from getting enough sleep at night, an excellent alternative is a regular daytime nap."[2]

Unfortunately many of us can't go home and crawl under the covers (although it certainly sounds tempting). We can, however, learn to take catnaps, those brief dropoffs to sleep that allow the napper to wake feeling refreshed and bright-eyed. Winston Churchill, John F. Kennedy, and Thomas A. Edison were just a few of the famous known for their ability at catnapping. Don't attempt it at work when the boss is looking, or while driving, of course, but if you perfect the art of catnapping, you may find yourself relaxed in a matter of moments. My cat does.

If, however, you find yourself constantly wanting to sleep, or actually sleeping during the night, albeit wakefully, and then during the day, too, you should see your doctor. You could be suffering from one of a number of physical disorders. You also, however, could be suffering from a mild depression yourself, brought on from the fatigue and concern of caring for someone who, despite all your love and effort, remains depressed. Studies show that "after a year of caregiving, most families reported changes in daily routine, and over one-third indicated that their health had suffered."[3]

Learning to relax is one way to preserve your precious energy and maintain a strong positive outlook. Your loved one's struggle with depression may take some time. Regular relaxation breaks will help you to remain supportive without becoming a shadow victim.

Endnotes

1. Elaine Fantle Shimberg, *Relief from IBS: Irritable Bowel Syndrome*, (New York: M. Evans & Company, Inc., 1988).
2. William C. Dement, M.D., Ph.D., "Daytime Sleepiness—Barrier to Good Health," © 1990 *Executive Health Report*, Vol. 26, No. 12; P.O. Box 8880, Chapel Hill, N.C. September 1990.
3. M. Adams, M.A. Caston, and B.C. Danis, "A Neglected Dimension in Home Care of Elderly, Disabled Persons: Effect on Responsible Family Members." Paper presented at the meeting of the Gerontological Society, Washington, D.C., 1979.

9

Maintaining Your Priorities

As I grow older, I've learned that many of my mother's old sayings—like "You can't do everything"—really make a lot of sense. Amazing how smart she's gotten over the years.

I'm like the girl in the song that has trouble saying no. Even armed with an outstanding assertiveness training course, I still waver and often accept responsibilities because so many things seem interesting. Then I wonder why I feel overwhelmed trying to juggle work, family responsibilities, caring for my home, organizational obligations, tutoring, recording "Talking Books," and something else that I can't remember so I spend a lot of time worrying over that and everything else I'm doing.

Your schedule probably is very similar. Almost everyone has a full and extremely busy life. But usually if you have a family member who suffers a heart attack, stroke, or is diagnosed with cancer or any of the other "socially acceptable" disorders, friends, acquaintances, and business associates are very willing to take over some of your responsibilities until you can handle them again.

It's different with depression. First of all, depression doesn't usually hit someone as suddenly as a stroke. It comes on less spectacularly. You often don't even recognize the signs at first, even though you begin to take over responsibilities that formerly were handled by the depressed person.

By the time you do understand what has happened, you may be swamped with additional obligations, plus the caregiving necessary to try to help the depressed person. You may be uncertain how to explain to others what's going on. Should you tell his or her boss about the depression or just make excuses? What about your friends? What explanation do you give to your kids and other family members?

Often, unfortunately, the decision is to say nothing. We still, even in the 1990s, have a medieval mentality when it comes to emotional illness. We're afraid what people will say, what they'll think, and how they'll feel about us. So we remain silent, suffocating in isolation under our burdens.

Yet the stress piles up, taking its toll on our own physical and emotional health. We must learn to set priorities in order to protect ourselves. Our first concern must be self-protection. Without it we're little help to ourselves or our depressed loved one.

Dr. Peter Dunne, a Tampa neurologist, told me of a woman who never left her sick husband's side while he was in the hospital. "He had suffered a major stroke," Dr. Dunne related, "and although he was very ill, I felt he had a good chance for a reasonable recovery. I urged the woman to go home to get some rest, to eat properly, to care for herself. She ignored my pleading. She wore herself out. Ironically she suffered a heart attack and died. There was no one else to care for her husband, and he had to be sent to a nursing home. If only she had kept her priorities straight."

The previous chapters have dealt with a number of ways in which you can—no, in which you *must*—care for yourself. Fatigue, despair, and lack of self-esteem all trigger depression as well as being signs of the disorder. Failure to take time to be good to yourself leaves you most vulnerable.

One of the most basic places to begin to set priorities is to eat right. Sounds so simple, doesn't it? But proper nutrition is the body's fuel. You wouldn't try a grueling road test without proper lubrication for your car's moving parts and a high grade of gas to power it. Yet many people attempt to cope with a loved one's grueling illness without maintaining even a basic minimum standard of proper nutrition.

Understandably it's hard to feel much like cooking, let alone eating, when there's such a scent of unhappiness in your home. Nothing tastes good, and what you do force down seems to stick in your throat. The face across from you at the table is such a portrait of sadness that food seems unimportant. But it isn't. Eating a balanced diet must become one of your top priorities. You need it to give you the strength to overcome and to handle the problems that come with a depression.

If mealtime is agony because your depressed family member just dawdles and listlessly shoves food back and forth on the plate, plan at least one or two meals away from him or her. Visit a friend or relative's house for lunch or tea, eat dinner out with a friend you haven't seen in a while, take a bag lunch to the park (a safe one) or to the pier and let Mother Nature entertain you with chatty squirrels, diving seagulls, or billowy clouds. Take some type of action that makes you aware of what you're eating and helps you to enjoy your meal, rather than just eating because you have to. Eating is supposed to be a pleasurable activity. Allow yourself the joy of it.

If you don't know what makes up a properly balanced diet, contact a registered dietician or nutritionist. Check with your local hospital or look in the Yellow Pages of your phone book. You also can write the national organization for names of those in your area:

American Dietetic Association
216 West Jackson Street, Suite 800
Chicago, IL 60606

There also are physicians and clinicians who have been specifically trained in nutrition. For a list of those in your area, send a stamped, self-addressed envelope to:

The American Board of Nutrition
9650 Rockville Pike
Bethesda, MD 20814

Now that you're eating properly, you may feel a little better, both about yourself and the "situation," as one woman called it. Now you can begin to inventory your responsibilities and activities and determine their priorities. Make a list of everything you have to do. Don't put them in any order just yet. Just list them.

You should have a lengthy list, ranging from "paying bills," "attending committee meeting," to "cleaning house" and "feeding the dog." You also should have some pleasurable events, such as "manicure," "plant flowers," and "aerobics class."

Once everything's listed, go back and read through the list. Mark those things that you really don't need to do or that someone else can do instead of you with the letter "D" for "delete" and "delegate."

Now's as good a time as any to go through the list of organizations to which you hold membership and weed out those that "no longer fit" or "are out of style." If in doubt, ask yourself:

1. Am I still interested in this organization's activities?
2. Does the group accomplish anything?
3. Do I have time (or money) to remain a member?
4. Do I enjoy being with the members?

If the answer to these questions is "yes," but you really can't attend all their functions or fulfill all the requirements, speak to the president. List those things you *can* do for the group and give assurance that you'll return to full participation as soon as you are able. Most clubs and organizations value working members too much to turn you out when you've expressed interest in remaining, but under these specific conditions.

Don't resign from all your clubs and organizations, however. You need to be around upbeat and happy people, so if a particular group offers just that, hold onto it. Depression in a family is an isolating force. Right now positive people are a healthy prescription for you to take and take seriously.

Read through the list again. Are there some things listed that take longer than they need to and are creating tension because you are procrastinating or trying for perfection? Mark these with the letter "S" for "start."

One of the reasons we procrastinate is that we *are* trying for perfection and, fearing that there's no way that the job will live up to expectations—ours as well as others—we put off beginning it. I've done that with writing assignments. Fearing that a book or article won't turn out as well as I want it to, I hesitate to get to work on it. A friend of mine puts off Christmas shopping because she worries she won't find the perfect gift. So she spends hours wandering through stores and returns home empty-handed. The week before Christmas she runs around buying what's left over from the early shoppers and gets angry with herself for procrastinating. We all know graduate students who have completed all their coursework but have not received their masters' degrees because they either can't start or can't complete their thesis because they fear it won't be "perfect," whatever that is.

When you keep putting off a task, you tend to carry it around as mental baggage, tucked into the "I have to . . ." section of your brain. As it builds up it tends to expand in importance. Too much crowded into this space can create great additional stress.

Study your list. Do you really have to wax the kitchen floor, or can it just be spot cleaned with a damp cloth? (Remember, nobody *really* eats off a person's kitchen floor. That's what dishes are for.) Do you have to write a report for your boss or would he or she really appreciate a succinct memo, which would save time for you both? Must you read all those magazines piled up in front of you or can you just skim the table of contents and clip those that interest you? Can you make those phone calls now and get them over with? Are they all really necessary or would a quick note do instead? Pare down a chore so you can accomplish it and get started working on it. It doesn't need to be perfect as much as it needs to get done.

Skim one of the many good books on time management—such as Alan Lakein's *How to Get Control of Your Time and Your Life* or Stephanie Winston's *Getting Organized*. Read them, however, not with the idea of learning to squeeze more into your already overworked day but rather to discover how to manage to do less.

Go back to your list. Rank the remaining items in the order of their importance. Put #1 on everything that must be done today. Include everything from both work and home. Carry the list in a small notebook or in your pocket calendar. Throw away all scraps of paper. Think: streamline.

Your #1 list might include "call doctor, get shirts at laundry, write draft of report, paste up newsletter, see Junior's hockey game, buy groceries."

Mark everything that must be done this week as #2. As the week progresses, these will eventually become #1 priorities, although you may discover by Friday that someone else is going by the laundry and can get the shirts or that the client cancelled the newsletter. If you have children, allow them to do some of the chores. We parents often misguidedly think we're doing the kids a favor to protect them from having to pitch in. The truth is they *know* something's wrong and would feel a lot less anxious if they were given something to do to help.

Your #3 priorities may never get done, but chances are that nobody will ever notice or care.

This is only my simple system, but it works for me and

has for others who have adopted or improved upon it. There are many other methods of priority ranking, some that work fine for many people and others that are so complicated that you spend even more time ranking priorities and NEVER get anything accomplished.

Remember, however, that life has a way of interfering with even the best of schedules. They're written to help guide you and aren't chiseled in stone. When my kids were little, the incidences of their getting sick always increased proportionately to the nearness of a deadline. Similarly when someone in your family is depressed, you can't predict moods or needs, and you will have to remain flexible in order to be available when needed.

I began this chapter with a bit of my mother's advice that was good. I end it with this refrain that wasn't: "Eat everything on your plate."

Not only was this poor advice for my waistline (and, to my knowledge, it never helped the starving kids abroad), but it also is poor advice for you who are trying to streamline your activities. There are some things on your plate that you should leave untouched, some projects that really don't matter all that much when compared to what you're trying to deal with right now.

Forget about putting those photos in albums; they're fine in the shoe boxes. You don't need labels on the file folders; just write right on the folders themselves. If no one else is willing to volunteer for a specific committee, maybe your group doesn't need that committee. Ask yourself, what happens fifty years from now if I don't do this?

There's a term used in racing called "drafting." It means that the runner, biker, or race-car driver gets behind another racer and eases up a bit while the one ahead blocks the wind. That's what you need to do just now. Determine your own physical and emotional limits. Don't compare with a relative or neighbor. It doesn't matter what theirs are; your physical and emotional limits are yours as much as your fingerprints are uniquely yours. Start today to set priorities that will help you to achieve what you must and are able to tackle, and coast a while.

10

What To Do When Your Child Is Depressed

"Children with depression." It almost sounds like a contradiction in terms. Childhood is supposed to be a magical time filled with laughter. Adolescence and the teenage years are fantasized by many as a carefree period with endless pink cotton candy, phone chatter, and convertibles. Kids aren't supposed to get depressed. But they do, and chances are, if you're reading this chapter, your child is one of those youngsters who *is* depressed.

You have my support and compassion. You're going through a very difficult period—it's trying for you, your depressed child, and for the rest of your family. It *will* get better eventually, even though right now you may not see any light at the end of the tunnel.

Having a depressed child turns your world upside down. You always thought things like this happened to other families, not yours. On the one hand you feel as though your child is trapped inside a glass bubble, and you can't reach him or her, no matter how hard you pound, scream, or search in vain for the opening. On the other hand you feel like a pin on a bowling alley, trying to avoid getting hit while around you everything else is toppling.

"It's not supposed to happen," you shout into the wind. Until recently experts might have agreed with you. Before the 1970s few people, professional or lay, realized that children, even babies as young as three months, could become depressed. Fortunately it is now widely understood that they can. Recent studies suggest that 2 percent or more of all children ages seven to twelve are seriously depressed. Many more suffer from transient depressions. Causes range from chronic illness to severe loss (which includes death of a parent), parental abuse, and loss of a close and meaningful friendship, to environmental and genetic factors.

Some researchers point to the high incidence of depressed children coming from families with depressed parents and suggest it is a learned response, that children respond to stress in their lives much in the same way that their parents do. When their parents react to pressure and frustration by becoming depressed, these experts say, the children will often respond as their role models do.

A study by *Teenage Magazine* reported that 76 percent of thirteen- to nineteen-year-olds surveyed said that pressure from school work and their environment caused their depressions. Difficulties with boyfriend-girlfriend relationships also was mentioned by 54 percent of the young people and family conflicts by 44 percent.

"There's no doubt that kids today are exposed to more stressors," said Tampa child psychiatrist Joseph Lupo. "I've been practicing for twenty-five years. Today I see four times as many depressed child and adolescent patients. Many young people have no extended family to go to for support if one or both of the parents are depressed. If a mother's depressed, for example, she can't give support and positive reinforcement to her children. Yet young people need that more today than ever before. The world gives you enough negative feedback. Kids depend on their parents for examples of how to handle disappointments, for tips on coping with life, for the knowledge that it's okay to have sad or angry feelings, that it's what we do with these feelings that is important. Unfortunately too often the parents didn't learn these things from *their* parents."

In addition to modeling parental behavior, many researchers suggest that depression is an inherited response, one that may be genetic. According to Gerald L. Klerman, M.D., Professor of Psychiatry at Cornell University Medical School and a world-renowned researcher and expert on depression, "Although depression is familial and may be genetically determined, current evidence does not support a specific mode of genetic transmission. . . ."[1] Dr. Klerman continues, "The nature of possible environmental risk factors is not established. The environmental risk factors could be biological, including changes in nutrition, the possible role of viruses, or the effects of an unknown depressogenic chemical agent in the water or air. Other environmental risk factors could be nonbiological: historical, cultural, and economic factors have been suggested. . . ."[2]

Studies presently being conducted by Dr. Klerman and others also hint that radioactive materials, such as radioactive iodine, may be a possible culprit as well.

If you're a parent of a depressed child, however, the "why" often gets mixed up with other emotions, including guilt for having done "something" wrong. Why else, you may ask yourself, would my child be so unhappy?

But stop blaming yourself for everything. While you may need to reexamine the way in which you and your spouse handle frustration and disappointment, or how you as a family communicate, as well as your parenting skills, it's unlikely that your child's depression comes solely from something you specifically did wrong. More than likely it stems from a series of unrelated events that pile up to trigger a depression in a youngster who also had a vulnerability toward depression.

"At first I just thought Terry was having trouble with his peers," a mother told me. "He didn't seem to have many friends, but I assumed it was because he was new to a school where all the popular boys were into sports. He's tall, like his father was, and a little awkward just now. But he's only fourteen. He'll grow into himself. Meanwhile, though, it's hard on him and on me. He stays in his room, speaks to his sister and me in monosyllables, and doesn't seem too interested in school. His grades have fallen off, and he doesn't seem to care. He was doing so well before we moved, when his father was still alive. Now it's as different as night and day.

"I had thought it would be better for us all to be in a town with other relatives, with some cousins around the kids' ages, but Terry makes no effort to be friendly with them. His sister resents his behavior. I think she may be a little jealous of the time I spend with him, too. Sometimes I feel like everything I've done since his dad died was wrong."

Yet, when talking further to the above woman, she admitted that her father had suffered from "black moods, when we kids all knew to stay away from him." The history of depression in her family, plus the loss of a parent, the loss of friends and prestige caused by changing schools, the low self-esteem due to lack of athletic prowess, and the youngster's own chemical makeup all may have mixed together to trigger this boy's depression. It was, as it usually is, a combination of factors.

Studies reveal that many depressed children lost their parents before they were thirteen. Many experts, however, also expand this sense of loss to include loss through separation rather than death, such as "losing" a parent through divorce, having one parent absent frequently through business travel or military duty, losing one's best friend due to a move, breaking up a romance, or having a close sibling marry and leave home or go off to college. The loss of a beloved family pet may also trigger a depression (in an adult as well as in a child).

If your child is depressed, you and your spouse probably find yourselves on an endless merry-go-round. Desperately you experiment with everything you can think of, from bribes to threats, to help your child feel better. You try not to blame one another for what might have caused the depression and work to avoid or deny resenting the time and energy you expend with the depressed youngster, often at the expense of the other children in the family, not to mention each other.

While fantasies of running away seem tempting, leaving the scene even for a brief respite often fails to bring relief. Both parents feel guilty, worry about what their depressed child might do in their absence, and end up talking about little else. No wonder that depressed children often have depressed parents.

Acting out behaviors

Often, especially with adolescents, depression wears a different face.

"I don't know why it took me so long to notice that anything was wrong," said Martha, mother of a sixteen-year-old anorexic. "I knew Diane was dieting, but she had been on many diets before. We both had. She wanted to lose about ten pounds, which would have been about right. It was winter and she wore sweatshirts and wool skirts, so I really hadn't thought much about her weight loss until I accidentally walked into her room and saw her in her bra and panties. I was shocked. She looked like someone with a wasting disease. She couldn't have been more than eighty pounds, yet she was getting dressed to go jogging. She assured me that she was fine and never felt better, that she was just trying to 'stay trim.'

"After that mealtime became an ugly tug-of-war. Her dad and I fussed at her to eat more, and she passively pushed food around on her plate until we'd scream. Then she'd jump up from the table, and we'd sit and stare at each other. It became a nightmare."

Anorexia and bulimia are only two forms of eating disorders that stem from poor self-image and a sense of hopelessness or loss of control. Overeating also reflects a youngster's feeling that he or she doesn't matter. Food becomes the weapon of choice in a dangerous battle between child and family. Unfortunately obesity in children may continue into adulthood with serious health risks.

Eating disorders are only one type of acting out behavior with a depression component. Drug and alcohol abuse, risk-taking, and sexual promiscuity are others.

An adolescent with a low self-image or feelings of angry rebellion may turn to the whispered promise of peace through drugs and alcohol in order to "feel good," even for an hour or so, not realizing that many of these "self-medication" drugs, including alcohol, are actually depressants and may cause an even deeper depression. According to Dr. Joseph Lupo, "Depression in teenage boys may often be acted out through alcohol use or fast and reckless driving."

Shoplifting, running away from home, and vandalism are other ways that young people act out their depression, desperately trying some form of action that might relieve them of their nameless, unending ache.

Similarly a teenager may find freedom from unbearable loneliness and a comfort in being held through promiscuous sexual intercourse, not recognizing that what really is being ignored are the underlying feelings of depression. It is no coincidence that teenage pregnancies and teenage sexually transmitted diseases are increasing along with teenage depression.

Each of these problems becomes a family problem because they have a rippling effect on the entire family, how it functions, and how its members see it as a unit. As with depression, you need to understand fully what each of these disorders is and how they affect your child as well as the entire family. Unfortunately there isn't space to address these most serious problems in this book. Check at your local library or bookstore for titles that may help to inform you.

While it's tempting merely to address the problem—that of drugs or alcohol or sex—it's necessary to treat the source of the problem, which often is depression. This is not a layman's job, even for a loving parent armed with the best of books. There are specialists trained to deal with your child's specific problems, so always seek professional help.

Stop making excuses and face the reality

It's hard to admit to yourself that your child—that once-adorable bundle of joy who filled you both with so much pride—is depressed. It's easy to make excuses. "Of course he's tired all the time. He's growing," or "I know she's moody, but all teenagers are."

Serious depression differs, of course, from the usual moodiness of adolescents trying to find themselves, and while fatigue is natural for a growing youngster who plays sports or otherwise is constantly on the go, it isn't normal for a young person who has withdrawn from those former activities and now just lies in bed, isolated behind the closed bedroom door. Feeling blue after breaking up a relationship or being cut from a team is expected, but when it continues for more than a few weeks or affects previous typical behavior, it becomes cause for concern. Chapter 3 describes what to look for in determining whether or not your child is depressed. If your youngster fits that description, it is most urgent that you and your spouse face up to it. Don't waste valuable time arguing with one another, making excuses, or trying to assign blame. The "why" is not as important as the "what to do now." Your child's life *could* depend on it.

Put teachers on the "team"

According to Elva Poznanski, M.D., Chief of Staff of Child Psychiatry and Professor of Psychiatry at Rush Presbyterian Saint Luke's Medical Center in Chicago, "Teachers, on average, do better than parents in recognizing depression in children."[3] They can be more objective and can benefit from observing firsthand the interaction between your child and his or her peers as well as any acting out behavior that may signal problems with depression. Teachers also, unfortunately, often see your child for far more waking hours a week than you do. Many youngsters feel more comfortable talking with a teacher or coach than a parent because it is a less emotional atmosphere.

If your child's teacher suggests that your child might be depressed, don't be resentful that the teacher is "interfering," or jealous that your child took the teacher into his or her confidence rather than you. Instead, thank your lucky stars that your young person has so caring and perceptive a teacher. Most teachers in America have far too many students crammed into their classrooms, are burdened with paperwork overload, and are underpaid. The fact that they also often serve as the first line of defense for youngsters with difficulties is a tribute to their dedication.

At the beginning of each new school year, take time to meet all your children's teachers, from kindergarten up through high school. Make them aware of any illness in the family, a recent death, or major change that might be creating unusual stress on your child.

When I learned that I had breast cancer, I contacted my children's teachers to let them know that I'd be undergoing surgery shortly with four weeks of radiation treatments following. The information helped the faculty to remain alert for any problems the kids might have had, understand any unusual behavior or lack of concentration, and in one case allowed for some special one-on-one communication between one child and a caring teacher.

The parent-teacher-child relationship triangle is a most vital one. For single parents, struggling to handle a double load of responsibility, teachers (including coaches and religious leaders) can serve as extra helping hands, broad shoulders, and listening ears, especially when you encourage their participation. Consider your child's teacher a ready ally, and arm him or her with important background information about your child and your family. Good teaching involves far more than shoving facts down a youngster's throat. Ideally it must begin with knowledge of each particular child in order to determine what educational technique works best.

Seek proper health care

If you suspect that something is wrong, that your youngster may be suffering from depression, don't wonder in silence and inaction. Pick up the phone and call your child's pediatrician or the family doctor to arrange for a complete physical. NEVER assume or try to make the diagnosis of depression on your own. There are numerous medical conditions—ranging from mild to serious—that present many of the signs listed for symptoms of depression. These disorders, which include mononucleosis, irritable bowel syndrome, colitis, anorexia nervosa and/or bulimia, diabetes, and brain tumor, just to mention a few, must be ruled out first. (Of course, a child can have any of these conditions AND be depressed as well.) The depression also could be related to drug or alcohol use. Once your physician is satisfied that there are no physical reasons for your child's symptoms, he or she will probably recommend a mental health specialist with experience in dealing with children—a psychologist, psychiatrist, psychiatric social worker, member of the clergy, or other professional—to meet with your child. This does *not* mean that the problem is all in your youngster's head or that your child is "crazy." It just means that he or she may be suffering from depression.

Don't take the diagnosis personally, either. The physician is not saying or even suggesting that you are a bad parent; he or she is saying that your child is suffering from depression *which can be treated* and needs to be seen by a professional in that field. If your child had diabetes or a broken ankle, you wouldn't hesitate to have it cared for by a specialist. Why hesitate when it's depression?

While it's possible that your adolescent may become upset when you tell him or her about seeing "a shrink," most young people are relieved that you, the adult, are going to get help for them. They understand that something's wrong but often can't express it. Some youngsters, however, refuse to go. "I'm not crazy," they shriek, slamming the bedroom door and locking it.

If this happens, stay calm. Refuse to negotiate. Tell your child very matter-of-factly that you understand his or her being afraid of this new experience, but that your responsibility as a parent is to take care of your children. This included arranging for inoculations when they were babies and getting treatment for all injuries and illnesses, including depression, until adulthood (and, often, long thereafter). Your reassurance that you don't see depression as some horrible stigma and that you understand it is not something the young person could just "shake off" if he or she tried should be comforting. So can your assurance that depression can be successfully treated. Deep down your child wants the help he or she knows is needed.

Although the therapist may meet first with your entire family, he or she will probably spend most of the time alone with your child. If you and your spouse are divorced, agree that this will *not* become an arena for you both to continue your disagreements. You're there because your child needs both of you. You both still have the responsibilities of parenthood, even if you don't live under one roof, so put on a united front. If you feel that you would like some time alone with the therapist to discuss personal issues, speak up. You may instinctively have insights to your child's behavior—or have knowledge about depression in your family background—that could help the therapist.

Be honest with these professionals. They may ask probing questions about your home life, your family's ways of handling frustrations and failures, parenting methods, whether or not anyone else in the family suffered from depression, and other things that seem quite personal. Be assured that they are not asking out of idle curiosity or because they are prying. They are trying to help your child and can only do so if you are truthful with your answers. This is not the time to try to gloss over family problems or to "look good" for the therapist. He or she is not judgmental. Besides, whatever you say, chances are good that the therapist has heard far worse.

While you shouldn't expect everything to be better after your child's had just one meeting with the therapist, you also shouldn't expect therapy to go on for years. Today's treatment usually focuses on "the here and now" and teaches people to cope with today's problems. Most sessions are planned with an end date in mind. Often, so-called "talk therapy" is combined with drug treatment as well. This will be discussed in detail in Chapter 12.

Don't be hurt if your child doesn't discuss what's going on in the therapy. Don't pry either. It's most important for the young person to realize that he or she can tell the therapist anything, and that it's being held in confidence. The professional will not share anything with you without your child's permission, with the possible exception of a youngster with suicidal tendencies. Your understanding of this issue will help everyone involved.

Actually, after a while, you may find that your youngster wants to talk about what he or she has learned in therapy. Follow the child's lead. Listen more than you talk. You might learn a lot as well.

You and other family members also may benefit from therapy sessions, as depression *does* run in families. For those who are not depressed, it could become a valuable preventive tool. For those who already are depressed, it is a means to understand depression more fully and learn ways to combat its vicious force. Both family therapy, in which the family meets as a group with the therapist, as well as individual therapy can be beneficial.

It's easy to point to the one member who is obviously depressed and say, "He's the one who's depressed, not me." But look within yourself. Unless you and other family members are treated as well, it may be difficult for the depressed member to keep from becoming "reinfected" whenever he or she is in the family grouping. The interactions of families—the very ingredients that make them so unique and rewarding—may also carry the seeds of destruction for the family as a unit, as well as for all the individual members. Never fear therapy. Knowledge *is* power, and the deeper understanding of depression and ability to know how to handle feelings, along with medical treatment when needed, can be powerful antidotes for this dubious and sometimes lethal legacy so often handed down from generation to generation like Grandma's silver candlesticks.

It is possible that your pediatrician or family practitioner may be one who still doesn't believe that children can be depressed. Studies reveal that 30 to 50 percent of depression is misdiagnosed. If, despite what your doctor says, your gut instinct tells you that your child is depressed, get another opinion. Doctors are only human and can make mistakes.

Listen to your kids

"I can't talk to my daughter," an acquaintance complained to me. "She just shuts me out whenever I try. How am I supposed to help her?"

I knew her daughter. She was tall for twelve, at that tough age where girls tower over the boys and search, in vain, for one who doesn't act like a jerk. After her softball practice she often joined me at my son's baseball games, where I was a faithful follower. She first had wandered over after practice because, having missed the bus, she needed a ride home and spotted me.

We talked about diets, how her classes were going, why boys her age seemed so infantile, and why zits appeared only on days that were important ones. Many days later she confessed that she often missed the bus because she really didn't want to go home any sooner than she had to.

"My mother asks questions and then keeps talking," she said. "I know she means well, but she's so busy talking at me that she doesn't hear what I'm trying to say. I just don't bother anymore."

I nodded thoughtfully. "It's a fault a lot of us have," I said softly.

Throughout baseball season we sat. Usually she talked and I listened. We did watch the game, too, I hasten to add, but often the most important play was that which was going on between the two of us on the bleachers.

It wasn't that I said anything so profound to her but that I listened. Twelve and thirteen, if you remember, are not the greatest of ages. Of course, I have only experienced them firsthand from a girl's viewpoint, but I have had a brother, have three sons, and have listened to numerous young men who confirmed that those preteen and early teen years are hard for boys as well. Youngsters at that age bond into cliques, which is great only if you're part of it. If you're not, it is horribly isolating and a verification of your major fear that something *is* wrong with you. Why? Because if there weren't, you would have been accepted into the club, gang, society, clique, or whatever you call it.

This was one of the problems she was struggling with. Along with suffering from peer rejection, this young lady didn't feel she could tell her mother that she was an outsider, that somehow she didn't fit in.

"My mother would be so upset," she explained. "All of her friends' daughters are in the 'Inner Circle' Club. How can I tell her that I didn't make it? I just said they weren't through tapping initiates yet."

Nobody likes rejection. My young friend admitted that

she felt depressed about being left out. When I answered that I thought that to be a most normal reaction, she agreed and seemed relieved. Being able to talk freely, without censoring her thoughts or feelings, she was soon able to accept that rejection happens to us all, that she felt depressed, but that she couldn't change the outcome. By recognizing and accepting her feelings, she was able to acknowledge the rejection and eventually was even comfortable enough to tell her mother (who was disappointed but not devastated as my young friend had feared), and then go on with her life. She confided that before we had started our bleacher-side chats she had felt lonely and depressed and had considered quitting the softball team. Now she was working even harder to become a starter at third base. "I just needed someone to listen," she said.

All kids need someone to listen. But it's hard for us to find the time and often even harder keeping our mouths shut and just listening. We're more experienced, we figure. We know the answers. Why won't they listen? Why won't they let us help them? Why do they shut us out?

We become impatient. But kids need time to express themselves. They usually can't just rush up to us and say, "I didn't get the part in the play, and I feel rotten." You need to give them the opportunity and encouragement they need. Words may come hard; emotions are new and painful when you're eight or ten or fifteen.

Children and adolescents who are suffering from depression have even more difficulty in expressing themselves. They're particularly sensitive to body language clues that reveal when you're pressed for time or when you're listening with only half an ear. They may hesitate to expose their deeper emotions when their siblings are around.

Plan for times when you can be alone, one-on-one, with your depressed youngster as well as with all of your children. It's better to say, "Johnny's coming home in a few minutes. Would you rather meet me by the swings in half an hour when we can be alone?'' than to hurry a conversation that may get suddenly broken off to both your dissatisfaction.

I always found running errands in the car to be particularly conducive to mother-to-child chats. You're driving, with your eyes on the road, so your youngster feels the comfort of a certain bit of anonymity, something like the privacy of the confessional where you don't actually have to look at the person you're talking to. In addition your kid is pretty much of a captive audience in a car—but remember you're there to listen, for the most part, not to talk. Turn the radio or tape deck off. Drive to the furthest spot first, even if it means having to double back to the cleaners later. Listen, and don't forget to nod or give verbal cues to let your child know you're listening.

If it isn't convenient to go for a drive with your youngster, make other time to be together in one-on-one privacy. Row the boat out to the middle of a lake, throw pebbles into the pond or feed the ducks, take a walk, or go into your bedroom and lock the door. A friend of mine gets out the flour and sugar when she thinks one of her brood needs to talk. They mix up a batch of chocolate chip cookies and she listens as the chips (and her child's resistance) melt.

Sometimes, of course, your child doesn't want to talk and *won't* talk, no matter how available you are. Respect that reticence while, at the same time, gently reminding your youngsters that you *are* available and are interested in what he or she has to say. Depressed youngsters have a very low self-image. Saying that you respect their wishes helps them to feel valued.

Often it isn't that your youngster doesn't want to talk to you, but rather that he or she is afraid to tell you something. Many young people conjure up expected reactions from their parents, and it is these fantasy expectations that they fear and that tend to make them mute. Often my kids would finally blurt out something and then be surprised at my reaction. "Gee, I thought you'd be mad," or "Aren't you disappointed?"

Remind them often that your love is unqualified; that you can be angry at them or disappointed in one of their decisions, but that you love them regardless. Until you have children it's difficult to understand the concept of how you can love someone simply because he or she is your child or, similarly, how you can love all your children "the same." Don't try to explain your feelings; just explain that they are there and that they are constant. Assure your children that you're there for them and encourage them to trust you.

Sometimes you may have to bite your tongue to keep from lashing back exactly as they had anticipated, but it's worth making the effort. Often, like a wader timidly testing the water, once your child has revealed just a little and found no outburst, he or she will dare to offer a little more. Before you know it you may have the beginnings of a real and valuable conversation.

Encourage "Mitzvah Therapy"

Psychologist Sol Gordon, educator and author of *When Living Hurts*, suggests that you introduce your child to "mitzvah therapy." According to Gordon, "I only know of two ways to promote self-esteem in young people. One is to teach them a new skill so that they have a sense of achievement, a pride in something they can do. The other is to get youngsters who feel miserable about themselves to do good deeds—mitzvahs—to be helpful to those in need of a helping hand."

While at first it may seem crazy, asking a child who feels depressed to reach out to someone else, it really can work miracles. According to Dr. Joseph Lupo, "You must insist on activity. Say that you're sorry they're hurting but that they need to do their part." Just getting a depressed youngster moving and thinking about someone or something other than him or herself can be of help.

"I bullied my son, Ronnie, to come with me for Meals on Wheels," Patti, a mother of four, told me as we sat together on a flight to New York. "He'd been depressed for months and nothing else had gotten him out of his room on weekends. After we delivered the first meal to a ninety-four-year-old-widow, he said, 'How can you do this kind of stuff? She's nothing but bones. She looks like she's been embalmed. And all she did was complain that you were a few minutes late.'

"I suppressed a sharp comeback and nodded. 'I'm the only visitor she has,' I told him. 'She has to let her emotions out on me because I'm all there is. I think she feels very unwanted. She's very lonely.'

"He was quiet as we drove to our next stop, but I could tell he was thinking. He could identify with that woman's feeling of frustration, her sense of total abandonment. The isolation which his depression had thrust on him was shared by this frail woman who suddenly had entered his life. The experience touched him in a way that I could not. He helped me with the remainder of my route. Although he didn't say much, I noticed that he seemed more responsive to each of my people. On the way home he asked when I was going again and offered to help me.

"Before long he and my ninety-four-year-old lady developed a real rapport. He actually got her to laugh. Now he stops by to see her often on his way home from school. She dresses up when she knows he's coming. He's also gotten his own group of Meals on Wheels recipients and has rounded up some of his classmates to pitch in. It's been his salvation, and I know all those young faces make the older folks feel good, too."

Depressed youngsters have low self-esteem and feel unworthy and unneeded, just like many of our senior citizens (who also may be depressed) do. They're too tired to move, or they take action in harmful ways, trying to dull their pain through sexual promiscuity, drugs and/or alcohol (which actually is a drug). What happens when you prod your youngster into volunteerism, when he or she comes to a day-care center to read at story time or help the little ones build block towers or dig holes in the sandboxes? Secretly watch as the toddlers throw their arms around your son or daughter to give an uninhibited hug, the unqualified soothing touch of love. That's definitely positive reinforcement, and it's bound to bring a smile to even the saddest of faces. Listen to your child's enthusiastic descriptions of trash gathered along a roadside or beach during a community cleanup day or of houses repaired and painted for the poor and elderly, and notice the animation in his or her voice and face. Giving to others *does* make you feel uplifted.

"We need to stop concentrating on what our kids *can't* do," said Dr. Sol Gordon, "and teach them something new. Give them alternate ways of coping. Get an outsider—an older relative or friend—to work with your child on throwing a ball, plucking at the guitar, training the dog, doing repair work, or painting once or twice a week. What it is doesn't matter, as long as it's a new skill removed from the usual doldrums. Then encourage your kid to share that new skill at the VA hospital, 'Y,' at a nursing home or day-care center. It's what I call the 'each one reach one' concept. We can't save the whole world, but we can save one person. And, as the Talmud says, when you save one person, it's as though you saved the world."

Think about it. What does your child do for others? In most homes it amounts to little more than taking out the garbage. Few schools have "community service hours" requirements; for many that do, it often is in name only. Is it any wonder that many youngsters have no sense of worth? Contrast that to the early part of this century, when children were needed to put in real labor in order to put food on the table. They *knew* they were needed; they had pride in a job well done.

There are, of course, those school administrations that

understand that "service to one's community" offers many positive rewards, including enhancing self-esteem and self-confidence and creating a sense of accomplishment for the students as well as benefiting the community. Rather than giving lip service to volunteerism, these schools assist the youngsters in locating or creating those programs that best fit their needs. Gonzaga College High School in Washington, D.C. and Jesuit High School in Tampa, Florida furnish student volunteers to help serve food to the homeless. At Tampa's Jesuit High School, additional students work with Habitat for Humanity, physically helping to dig foundations and hammering nails to help build homes for the needy. The 650 boys in this school donate an average of 26,000 hours annually to various community service projects.

"Their attitude on community service is positive and accepting," said Elliott Egan, Ed.D., the school's former director of community service. "Their written conclusions in the end-of-the-year summary usually include something like, 'I never would have done community service without having to, but I'm glad it was a requirement.' Our boys have ownership over the particular project they select. It gives them a feeling of control over their lives and a sense of pride in accomplishment. The total and involved support from our school's adult leadership plays a vital part in the students' acceptance of community service as a valued commitment."

No child is too young to gain from the self-esteem that comes from helping others. Recognizing this, many elementary schools have set up peer tutoring programs, in which fourth and fifth graders help first and second graders with reading skills. Not only do the little ones improve their reading, but the older children, some of whom may have begun to show behavioral problems, develop pride in their accomplishments and become more self-disciplined and demonstrate positive signs of leadership.

In San Antonio, Texas, potential dropouts were selected to help tutor younger students. Not only were they successful as tutors, but their own grades and behavior improved and the dropout rates declined. Mitzvah therapy works.

If your child's school doesn't encourage volunteerism and in-school or community service projects, promote them. As Dr. Egan put it, "Service to others makes a person feel good about him or herself. It exercises your soul, like jogging exercises your body."

Hold regular family meetings

I've always been a believer in family meetings. When my five children were young, each fall, before the school year began, my husband and I called a family meeting. The kids brought their allowance requests in writing, showing how they had planned their budgets; we discussed rules, curfews, problems, whether to get another dog (no), if the cats could be inside cats (yes), and plans for the next family vacation.

Now that they're grown, our meetings are less structured. We tend to hold them at our regular Sunday night dinner out (usually Oriental), with as many kids in attendance as possible. It's a time for sharing news of everyone's week, asking whoever borrowed the video camera to please return it, and to laugh as much as possible. What we discuss is really not as important as the fact that we do still set aside time to talk as a family.

One of my children (late twenties, but one's kids are *always* one's children, regardless how old they become) said this about family meetings: "It's a great way to get everyone's input. Often it becomes a creative brainstorming, like we have in our work place."

It's especially important to have these meetings when you have a depressed family member. It gives everyone a chance to learn more about depression and to try to understand its force. It helps to reduce the sense of anger and embarrassment that often develops in families with a depressed family member. Knowing the facts about depression may offer important emotional support to children and teenagers who may be especially frightened by the change in their parent, sibling, or other relative and not know what to expect or how to respond.

These family meetings allow time for discussion about fears any family member may have, an interchange of ideas on what seems to work or not work, and requests for specific help in different situations.

"I just felt swamped," a young mother confessed, "trying to take care of our kids as well as my mother who was depressed and taking up more and more of my time. The only answer seemed to be to have Mother move in with us, which I really didn't want to do. We held a family meeting. One of the kids came up with the idea of having a weekly picnic at Mother's apartment. They prepared the food, packed it in a hamper, and we all went over to Mother's, spread out a blanket, and had a terrific picnic—without ants. I even think Mother began to look forward to it. It was just a small thing, but it made a difference to all of us. The kids felt they helped out with Nana, and it was fun for us to know we could look forward to one day a week to relax a little.

"My husband and I had been so busy trying to cope with Mother's depression on top of all of our other responsibilities that we had sort of let the fun aspect of living slide by. We also had tried to shield the kids from this particular problem and hadn't realized that, rather than protecting them, our actions had made them feel shut out of a family issue. They were confused and a little resentful. Why didn't we want their help? Didn't we think their ideas were important? Didn't we think *they* were important? The family meeting cleared the air and helped us put laughter back in our life; to stay, I hope."

When there has been illness in our family, we have shared the information, speaking frankly about treatments, side effects, and possible outcomes. We talked about how the illness would affect us as a family, what everyone could do to help, and how it made us feel. Our kids have had a chance to ask questions, express fears, and allowed us the chance to offer reassurance. Now that most of our children are grown, my husband and I have often been on the receiving end of that comfort and reassurance as well.

Family meetings also can be a time to let the depressed youngster know how his or her behavior affects the rest of the family. Often the withdrawal or acting out through reckless behavior, promiscuous sexual activity, and/or drugs and alcohol has isolated the young person from the family. It may actually come as a surprise to him or her to discover that the other family members are hurting, too. Once siblings and parents share their feelings and the depressed child sees that the roof hasn't caved in or the sun failed to shine, he or she may be able to let down the guard and express some of his or her emotions in the safety of a caring family circle.

Adopting family meetings forces you all to set aside a specific time for interaction and communication among the family members. Sometimes, to be honest, little is actually solved or achieved, but the feeling of camaraderie and the emphasis the meeting places on the importance of the family unit makes it worth the time and effort. It strengthens everyone's sense of belonging.

Set up specific rules for your family meetings. Be sure that everyone understands them and follows them. They might include some of the following:

- Our family meetings will be held on the first Sunday night of every month at 7 P.M.
- Extra meetings may be called by any family member.

- Meetings will be conducted by Father (or Mother), but all members will be allowed time to speak on every issue.
- Honesty of feeling and openness is encouraged, although rules of common courtesy must be followed.
- No one may speak while someone else is speaking.
- Brainstorming and creative thought is encouraged.
- Family members will show respect to one another throughout the meeting, regardless if they agree with what's being said or not.
- Decisions will be made on a majority basis, with parents having the right to veto if deemed absolutely necessary (such as the children voting to take a family trip to Europe or getting a new pet).

It's altogether possible that your depressed child will sit at your meeting looking bored and withdrawn. Don't let it keep you from holding your meetings. The rest of your family can still benefit and may even want to air their feelings about and to the depressed person. You can force attendance at these meetings but not attention. Often, however, your young person is tuning in to more than you may think. He or she may surprise you by speaking up on one or more issues.

You sometimes may discover that you have to face issues *you* hadn't wanted to face. Once one of the kids asked if we had ever failed at something. It surprised us. Then we thought about the question. We always had shared news of our successes but had kept our failures to ourselves. It was a mistake. Young people need to know that failure is part of life and learning. Failures should become important teaching aids. We talked that night of mistakes we had made and failures we had experienced both at their ages and recently. It made us seem more human; we had shared experiences and feelings. It also lifted the burden of trying to be perfect from their shoulders. Many youngsters who are depressed feel that they are useless because they keep making mistakes; we need to share our failures if only to remind our children that the only people who never make mistakes are at the cemetery.

Family meetings also serve to keep you aware of both sides of an issue. It's easy to say no or make rules without thinking them through. Give the kids a chance to be heard so you can see things from their perspective.

All of our kids have had curfews. The boys complained from time to time that "none of the guys have curfews," but we held fast. "They live at their house; you live at yours," we told them. Our youngest one took the floor one night at the family meeting to complain about his curfew.

"I'm a junior, and my curfew is earlier than most of the freshman or sophomore girls I take out." We considered the problem and had to admit that his early curfew had been for *our* convenience. We got tired and went to bed after the news. It was hard for us to stay up any later. But he was right. We raised his weekend curfew and learned to watch and sometimes enjoy *Saturday Night Live*.

Family meetings give youngsters a feeling of being empowered. They not only learn to stand up for their rights, but they also learn the art of compromise. They discover how to express themselves concisely and effectively. They receive positive feedback about their judgment and creative thinking ability and learn responsibility. These are valuable assets in helping a young person to feel confident and to raise his or her self-esteem.

You may feel a little self-conscious at first when you mention to your family that you'd like to organize regular family meetings. You also may meet with resistance and protests of, "I'm too busy." But try it. You'll find that it's a lot like exercise: difficult to get started, but you feel so much better when you make it a regular habit.

Will all these things—improved communication, sharpening skills through volunteering, family meetings, sharing both good and bad experiences—keep your child from becoming depressed? Not necessarily. As mentioned before, depression is triggered by many factors. But strengthened family ties, a strong sense of confidence and self-esteem, and an ability to communicate desires and feelings can often turn a youngster who feels depressed to seeking help before the depression is so deep that it becomes overpowering and more difficult to overcome.

Remember that the early signs of depression in children often are different from those of adults. If you've forgotten what they are, go back and re-read that section of Chapter 3. Without badgering your child or driving him or her crazy by hovering or analyzing every word and move, be alert for changes that signal depression, and act on your hunches. Your doctor and the therapist must make the diagnosis, but you, as parent, will probably be the first to suspect. Don't let well-meaning friends and family help you rationalize away your fears. Denial comes easy. Just remember that depression is the only psychiatric disorder that is potentially fatal: suicide is the third leading cause of death in adolescents (over ten thousand youngsters each year). Accidents are listed as the second leading cause of death, and many of these actually may be suicides as well.

Childhood is not as we fantasize it, carefree and filled with constant fun and laughter. Depression in children is real. It can be treated, but first it must be detected.

Endnotes

1. Gerald L. Klerman, M.D., "Prospects for the Future," *Suicide and Depression Among Adolescents & Young Adults*, ed. Gerald L. Klerman (Washington, D.C.: American Psychiatric Press, 1986), p. 370.
2. Ibid.

3. Elva Poznanski, M.D., "Depression in Children and Adolescents: An Overview," *Psychiatric Annals*, vol. 15, No. 6, (June 1985): p. 465.

11

Twelve Ways You Can Help a Depressed Loved One

In his recent nonfiction book *Darkness Visible: A Memoir of Madness*, author William Styron described his tortured feelings while suffering from serious depression, comparing his illness to physical pain so unforgiving that death seemed the only way out. Likening it to "drowning or suffocation," Styron wrote, ". . . the pain of severe depression is quite unimaginable to those who have not suffered it, and it kills in many instances because its anguish can no longer be borne."[1]

While Styron's book is important because it describes in exquisite detail the agony of being caught in the web of a serious depression, it offers only passing reference and tribute to the family members who also suffer but from the sidelines. The pain of those who love but are helpless to heal is seldom mentioned in most books on depression; indeed, that was the motivational force behind this one.

Your suffering may be almost as great, as tormented, because with it comes the frustration of failure to rid your loved one of this plague along with guilt in wondering what you possibly might have done to trigger it. You experience the agony of losing a loved one, not through the finality of death, but through isolation inflicted by the depression. It is a separation of both the spirit and physical body. It is as though you stand on

154

one iceberg watching helplessly as on another your lover, friend, companion, child, or parent drifts away from your grasp, leaving you clutching only frigid air. Knowledge that depression may have a genetic basis may only heap additional guilt on parents when their child is depressed.

Your patience and energy levels falter. You experience a fatigue as great as that created by depression. You wonder if this curse will ever be lifted.

The good news is that in most cases depression *will* eventually go away, although it often does recur throughout the person's lifetime. The bad news is the reality that it takes time for depression to lift.

While "talk therapy" is, for the most part, no longer a process requiring many years' investment, one visit does not cure someone who's depressed. Likewise one pill won't, like a mother's kiss, make "everything all better" either. Frequently the doctor must change medications one or more times until he or she finds the specific drug that works on a specific patient. Each medication also must be tried for a number of weeks in order to see if it is effective before abandoning it and trying something else. Dosage also must be titrated for each specific individual.

Finally time, pure and unadulterated time, must pass before the depressed person is able to sleep in peace once again and function normally in his or her waking world. Patience, that virtue you've heard so much about, must be your constant companion.

You're there for the long haul when someone you love is depressed. It helps to know that in advance because it lets you pace yourself and understand why so much of this book deals with how you can make yourself feel better. You're going to need those relaxation techniques; you're going to need to spend time with people who make you laugh and feel good about yourself if *you* aren't to become depressed as well.

This chapter lists ways that you can help a depressed

loved one. The important word here is "help." You won't be able to cure, threaten, or cajole, but you can help.

1. Learn all you can about depression

Knowledge is vital to help you dispel the myths about depression and to understand what is happening to the person who is depressed, to yourself, and to the rest of the family. It's also important to have this information because you probably are going to be the one to help the depressed person make some decisions. The more you understand depression, the more educated your decision.

Unfortunately, like many things, most of us aren't too interested in depression until it knocks on our door. We might know or hear of someone who is depressed and feel sorry, but without understanding much about depression we might privately think that "good old Joe would be fine if he just stopped feeling sorry for himself," or that "Aunt Betty would snap out of it if she just got up and got dressed." Once we understand the facts concerning depression, however, we know that the person cannot feel better about himself because he *is* depressed, and that the depression makes him feel unworthy and unwanted.

Once we understand depression we know not to accept it as a normal condition and especially not to excuse it among the elderly by saying, "Well, he's old. Naturally he's depressed." We know that Aunt Betty can't get up and get dressed because the effort involved in taking off her nightgown and then having to decide what to put on is so horrendous that it exhausts her. She literally can't face making that decision. Once we understand depression, a light goes on and, like a monster in the corner exposed to be no more than our sweatsuit, we lose our fear of depression and can reach out with confidence.

2. Offer continuing unqualified support

This often is easier to say than do. You're only human. You eventually grow tired always being the cheerleader, especially to an unresponsive audience.

"I sometimes feel like Pollyanna," the wife of a depressed bank executive told me. "I'm constantly telling Jack that he looks wonderful, assuring him that I won't leave him, reassuring him that I love him. It feels as though everything is going out and none of it's coming back. Intellectually I know that he can't help it. I can accept that he's depressed, but emotionally it sure would be nice if someone told *me* I looked nice and that I was loved."

The reality is that the depressed person needs you to reaffirm his or her existence. Like a too-clingy child, he or she needs reassurance that you'll be there, that you can handle everything, that you know all the answers, that you care, that you still feel love for him or her. The depth of this feeling of being unlovable is so great that it seems unbelievable to the depressed person that you *could* love, could care, so you must offer reassurance repeatedly. It tries your patience at times. You feel exhausted with all the additional responsibilities placed upon you just now and a little resentful that, no matter what you do or say, the depression just hangs on.

Don't give up, though. You may be the only oasis. You may offer the only hint of hope in the depressed person's world, which seems inhabited only by hopelessness. It's a heavy load to carry.

3. Simplify life

Think of yourself in slow motion trying to function in a world that's whirling around you. That's the problem for the depressed person. He or she cannot concentrate, cannot focus, not on what you say, not on the job at hand, not on anything. It's like having a pain so blinding that everything else ceases to exist.

Help the depressed person by reducing some of the

clutter in his or her life. In doing so, you also help min-imize the number of decisions that must be made. Re-member how it was when you first taught your toddler to have confidence in his or her decisions? You didn't ask your child what shirt he or she wanted to wear. Instead you brought two out of the dresser and said, "Would you like to wear the red shirt or the blue?"

Do the same for your depressed family member. For example, rather than asking your depressed father, "What should I bring over for dinner tonight?" make a simple statement of fact. Say "I'm bringing dinner over at five." In the first place, if he's depressed, he has no appetite anyway. Food seems unimportant, so there's no use try-ing to have him make a decision about food. Just tell him. He'll probably nod and wave a hand as if to say, "Whatever."

Use shorter sentences, and speak more slowly, too. A depressed person's mental processing time has slowed down like everything else, from the digestive system to decision-making abilities. Don't talk down to someone who's depressed or speak too slowly, though, or the de-pressed person may give up listening altogether. De-pressed adults are still adults; if you talk down to them with the maddening speech form used by stereotypical kindergarten teachers and nurses—"Well, did we have a nice nap?"—you will only reinforce their already exist-ing feelings of being helpless and unworthy.

Try to prevent cross talk at the dinner table and other family gatherings. It's difficult enough for a depressed person to concentrate on what one person is saying; if two or more conversations are going on at once, a usual happening at dinner or family gatherings, the depressed member may withdraw even more.

Clear away clutter from throughout the house, includ-ing desktops and countertops, too. Your depressed loved one already feels overwhelmed and that life is hopeless. If there's a stack of unfolded laundry or unpaid bills star-ing back from the table, it could dangerously multiply those feelings. Yes, it probably means that *you* are going to have to fold the laundry and pay the bills, along with doing most of the housework, cooking, and child care. There's no getting around the fact that having someone in your family who is depressed means more work for those who aren't.

Before you begin to get depressed yourself just thinking about all the extra work and responsibilities, consider this: Simplifying life for your depressed loved one has an extra benefit for the rest of the family. In addition to making it easier for the depressed family member to function in the household, it also cuts down and cuts out a great deal of unnecessary work and energy expense for you and the other family members. As a matter of fact, you all may choose to keep life a little simpler when the depression eventually is gone, too.

4. Don't try to "manage" the depressed person's depression

When you're the caregiver, it's easy to see what needs to be done to help the depression. It seems so simple to you. That's because you're not depressed. But the depression belongs to the person who's depressed and not to you. You can't make them happy or make it go away no matter how hard you want it to or how frantically you try.

Parents of children with diabetes, hemophilia, and cancer are warned by their offspring's doctors, nurses, and social workers that they must let their child handle his or her own disease. It is the child's disease, not the parent's disease. It's the same with depression. You cannot *make* someone want to be helped; you can drag them bodily to the doctor, but unless the depressed person allows the doctor to treat him or her, you'll only end up feeling more frustrated, more rejected, and eventually depressed yourself.

In her book *Codependent No More*, author Melody Beattie warns against becoming a "codependent,"

which, as she defines it, is "a person who has let someone else's behavior affect him or her, and is obsessed
with controlling other people's behavior."[2]

It's easy to say, of course, but much more difficult to
achieve when you love someone and you have such empathy. You *want* to help; you want to make the depression
go away so things can go back to the way they were. But
you must let go. Support, yet let go. It sounds like a
contradiction, but it isn't.

5. Make time for yourself

Every expert interviewed for this book offered identical advice: "Tell the family members to make time for
themselves. If they don't, they'll become depressed as
well."

That's why so many chapters in this book deal with
what you need to do for yourself. You'll be no earthly
good for your loved one if you become physically exhausted, lowering your immunity and making you more
susceptible to illness, or if you become depressed yourself.

At least once a week have lunch with a friend who
makes you laugh. You'll be amazed how good you feel
afterward. During the writing of this book, I discovered
that, from time to time, I felt depressed myself. It wasn't
the burden of the approaching deadline; I've been a writer
for almost thirty years and never missed one. It wasn't
simply the material; I've written about sad subjects before. Perhaps it was that I wanted this book to be useful,
a supportive tool for families struggling with a depressed
member. Sometimes I felt overwhelmed with the task.
There's so much to be included; each chapter could be a
book in itself.

I put my own advice into practice and every few weeks
called five "funny friends" to set up lunch dates. No,
these weren't professional comedians, just friends who
are upbeat, positive, and who see life with a "twinkle."
They've experienced sad times, of course; no one gets

through life without those. But basically they are happy people, who see humor even while they're crying and laugh at absurdities even while they're trying to cope.

I made lunch dates with these friends to help me feel good. For an hour each day I was recharged by their positive energies. It was like having a mood transfusion. No, I didn't feel badly about "using" them. I've done the same for them. Friends do that for each other. I returned to work feeling upbeat and energized. From time to time I also bought myself a bouquet of flowers. The message was "You deserve it!" Did these gimmicks work? You bet they did. Try them.

Not only do I encourage you to be with positive people; you also should try during these troubled times to stay away as much as possible from what I call the "Down 'n' Frown Folks," people who begin every sentence with "I'm so irritated . . ." or "I'm just furious that . . ." or "I hate . . ." These folks have their own problems as well, but their negativity can rub off on you. Before you realize it you start competing in a negative pyramiding of "Isn't it awful," sort of a "Can You Top This?" of negativism. Experts say depressed people seek each other out, so stay away from these depression carriers. Inoculate yourself with positive thoughts instead.

Also make yourself feel good physically by beginning and maintaining a regular exercise program, learning and practicing relaxation techniques, and eating a balanced diet. Don't look to alcohol or other drugs to give you the boost you need. Most of them are actually depressants and will only serve to drag you down.

6. Deal with your emotions

When someone you love is depressed it's very easy to keep so busy that you literally don't have time to think. You may consider that a benefit, but it isn't. Running from the pain is not the same as learning to deal with it. It's only denying its existence.

Don't be afraid of your feelings. It's not a sign of

weakness to admit that you're angry. You're not "awful" if you sometimes wish the depressed person would just disappear and leave you alone. Sometimes you even— dare we mention it?—wish he or she would die. That's not an abnormal thought, so don't feel you're some horrible ogre to think it. Wishing *won't* make it happen, so let go of your guilt.

As you learn about depression, you may intellectually understand that your husband's refusing to shave or get dressed is because of his illness, and not that he's trying to get back at you for some reason; or that his sitting all day in silence is not to punish you, but is because he is so deeply depressed. Nevertheless, being human, you may feel terribly hurt, upset, and frustrated that you can't seem to do anything to help. So admit it. You'll feel better.

"Take your feelings out of the closet," urges psychologist Joseph Lupo. "Talk about them. Create an environment at home where it's okay to have feelings. Urge your schools to teach feelings to their students."

Imagine a history class in which emotions were part of the lesson: "What would it have been like to face your brother in battle during the Civil War?" A discussion takes place, with kids talking freely about sibling rivalry, a mother's pain in having two sons in battle against one another, how we feel about 'home' and 'country.' Picture an English class in which the emotional makeup of the characters was as important as the plot.

How are you expressing *your* feelings? What are you teaching your children about expressing theirs? You can help your depressed family member, too, by admitting when you feel frustrated, angry, overwhelmed, or worn out. Demonstrate that you can express these feelings without serious repercussions. The depressed person may take your hint and begin to show a little of his or her feelings.

It may be difficult for you, however, to say what you feel to others when you haven't even admitted it to yourself. Keeping a private journal is a good way to express your thoughts. It's a beginning in learning to acknowledge your feelings before you really feel comfortable in expressing them aloud.

Share your feelings with a friend who you feel will not betray your confidence. Don't overload on them, however or *they'll* start to feel depressed as well. You might feel more comfortable talking with a trained professional—a member of the clergy, psychologist, social worker, your physician, a psychiatrist, teacher, or any of the empathetic professionals who are trained to encourage expression of emotions and to help you handle them.

One emotion common to families of depressed people isn't easily recognized at first. It sort of creeps up on you and envelops you before you can identify it. It's called loneliness.

When someone in your family is depressed, your world often grows smaller. The family "circles the wagons" and closes in to protect the depressed member. The kids stop inviting their friends over; you pull away from your friends because you really don't want to talk about "it." Your actions, however, only add to your sense of isolation.

If your spouse is depressed, you may hesitate to go out socially. He or she doesn't want to go, doesn't feel "up to it," and you feel selfish wanting to go out alone, thinking that your place is with him or her. You also may feel uneasy going out by yourself, worrying about what might happen to your loved one alone at home. So you stay home, too, keeping guard, watching reruns on television. Your concern and empathy slowly evolve into anger and frustration; but out of loyalty and love, you keep quiet.

Your old friends drift away because it's not much fun being around someone who's depressed. You understand but that doesn't make the loneliness any easier to bear.

Help the depressed person by gently urging him or her to do things with you. Activity is the key. Anything that gets you both moving and around people—a walk in the park, stroll through a shopping center or art museum, or trip to the beach—will help the feelings of being isolated. Too much stimulation may be overwhelming, so go gradually.

Volunteerism, as mentioned before, may help you both by reaching out to others. It's hard to feel lonely when you're holding a little hand in a day-care center or reading to a sightless senior citizen in a nursing home.

Sometimes, however, you do feel lonely for the relationship that existed before the depression took hold. Tell your loved one that you miss it and that you look forward to reconnecting again soon. Share that honest feeling while at the same time offering hope for the future. The depressed person sees no future, no light at the end of the dark tunnel. You must believe in it and provide it for him or her.

7. Ask for help

We're proud, many of us. Our mantra, "I can do it myself," was instilled in us at our mother's knee. So we struggle on, carrying unnecessary burdens, and shake our heads when others ask if they can help. Soon, all too soon, they stop asking.

Sometimes we don't ask for help because we don't know exactly what we need help with. We're so loaded down with worries over our loved one who's depressed, the additional responsibilities of all that's been dumped in our laps, and the fear that we're forgetting something, that we haven't stopped to think what others could do to make things easier.

Friends want to help when they know you're having problems, but *they* don't know what to do either. So you both do an uneasy dance. They don't want to interfere or intrude; you're embarrassed to let them know what's going on behind closed doors. They're frustrated; you're exhausted.

So let people help you. You don't have to do it all

yourself. Tell your friends what you need and be specific. ''Could you drive my morning car pool for the next few weeks?'' ''May I leave Johnny at your house Wednesday afternoons when Tom sees the doctor?'' ''How about staying with Dad for an hour a week?''

You don't need to share all the intimate details of your family member's illness, of course, but don't try to keep the problem a secret out of some sense of loyalty. There's no disgrace in having a depressed member of the family. Besides, chances are that your friends already know.

Allow yourself to accept the emotional support you need from friends at this moment. You're probably not getting it from your loved one, who's struggling just to make it from day to day. By asking for help from others, you relieve your loved one from any guilt or worry that you're being neglected. He or she may recognize that you're lacking the emotional support you need right now but has nothing left over for you. That doesn't mean that this will be the situation forever, but to be blunt, it is for now. So open to your friends and let them help. It isn't being disloyal to your depressed family member; it's letting friends help. Don't be ashamed to ask and don't get discouraged if you ask a friend for help and he or she doesn't follow through or helps once and drops out. Don't operate on the assumption that everyone will act that way.

8. Be firm

Sometimes you can help someone who is depressed by being firm. At times it may seem unnecessarily harsh, but it isn't. It offers a support to someone who needs something unbending to lean on, to bolster him or her up until the depression eases and balance returns. Just as children need to know how far to go, depressives also are helped by knowing that someone has set parameters for them.

It is especially important to be firm when someone has bipolar depression and is in the manic stage. If you don't keep control of the checkbook, for example, you may find yourself in the position of one woman who discovered the family bank account empty and her garage filled with tires. Her husband, in a manic state, had figured he would corner the market on tires and have Detroit car manufacturers crawling to him. She was eventually able to return them all, but not without much effort and expense.

Be firm about appointments, too. It is easy for someone who is depressed to stay in bed rather than keep an appointment with the doctor or therapist. While you can't force someone to be helped, you need to remind your family member firmly that he or she agreed to make the appointment and that the doctor or therapist expects it to be kept.

When it comes to family get-togethers, encourage the depressed person to join in. He or she probably won't want to. "You'll have a better time without me. I'm no fun," you'll hear. Depressed people feel that they don't have anything worth saying and that no one really could enjoy their company. Don't try to force it, but leave the offer open. If you're all ready to go and the depressed person isn't even dressed, say that you're sorry and go. If you stay home too, you'll only add to his or her guilt and deepening depression. (If you're concerned for the person's safety, of course, have someone come to keep him or her company.)

It's often hard to be firm with someone who's depressed, because you feel you should do whatever you can to make him or her feel better; but it's important that you remain firm for the person's sense of security. Depressed people have difficulty in making decisions, so they rely on you to set the rules for them. Don't waver. You may be the only beacon guiding your loved one out of harm's way.

9. Become aware of medication needs

In many cases depression is treated by drug therapy in addition to talk therapy. It's important for you and other family members to become aware of each type of drug prescribed, what it looks like, what it's supposed to do, and what the side effects may be.

Although it's important for the depressed person to take responsibility for his or her depression and any medication that has been prescribed, often the depression itself makes it difficult for the person to remember what has been prescribed and how often to take it. He or she may not be the best judge of the effectiveness of the medication and/or the existence of any side effects. While Chapter 12 will discuss types of treatment for depression in more detail, be aware that you can be of great help to your depressed family member by becoming knowledgeable of his or her medications, understanding the possible side effects, and being supportive if and when they occur.

Offer encouragement and reminders to take the proper dosage, not by nagging, but by helping to come up with a system of containers or charts so that the depressed person can remain in control of the treatment. If, however, you're concerned in any way about the possibility of a suicide attempt, then you obviously must take responsibility for doling out the medication. Many antidepressant drugs can be lethal if an overdose is taken.

10. Rely on professional advice

If you've ever had any kind of illness, you may have been amazed at the amount of unsolicited medical advice you received from everyone from taxicab drivers and elevator operators to hair stylists and relatives. Everyone's an expert.

The problem with this kind of advice is that much of it is based on myths and mistakes. In addition, even physicians and other professionals often disagree among themselves about which specific type of treatment is most effective. So how do you know what to do? How do you know which treatment is best for your loved one?

As mentioned earlier in this chapter, you must learn

as much about depression as possible. Then you'll know that it isn't true that someone could just snap out of depression if he or she tried, or that you can always tell if someone is suicidal. You'll stop accepting advice from the man on the street.

"I did an awful thing to my son," a father confessed to me. "A guy I work with kept at me about being too easy on my boy, said that he needed to toughen up a little. I knew Johnny was depressed about being cut from the basketball team, but instead of letting him talk about it, I said I didn't want to hear another word. I taunted him about learning to be a man, that real men don't cry, and all that other nonsense. I withdrew from him just when he needed me most. Not long after that Johnny ran the car into a tree. I almost lost him. Why I took advice from someone who didn't know what they were saying I'll never know. Thank God, I got a second chance."

Learn the facts about the enemy. Then put your trust in those professionals who have had experience in dealing with someone who is depressed. They may have differences of opinion, however, and you, along with the depressed person, if possible, and other family members will have to make some decisions concerning whose professional advice to take, based on what you have learned.

In addition, there are many experts who can help. Because they are human, just like you and me, there may be personality differences and in some cases personality clashes. Here again, trust your instincts. If your family member doesn't like, trust, or feel comfortable with a particular therapist or other professional, find another.

Read more about what treatment is available for those suffering from depression in Chapter 12.

11. Remain alert for suicidal threats and attempts

Depression is the only psychological disorder that is potentially fatal. Its pain is so great that for many depressives suicide seems the only way to find relief.

Chapter 13 deals exclusively with what to do when a loved one talks of suicide. Read it carefully and remain ever watchful. Do not believe the myth that says people who talk about committing suicide won't try it; they *do* try it, and many succeed.

On the other hand, many depressed people never speak openly about suicide. They just quietly plan it and carry it out. Nobody likes to think about suicide, much less the possibility that someone they love may be thinking about it. This is no time to hide your head in the sand, however. Learn what you should do and remain alert.

12. Look for the light

There is an end to most depressions, even though it's hard to imagine when you as a family are struggling with the effects of it. It's important to remember this, however, and to keep reassuring your depressed family member. He or she is so dominated by the pain of the depression that life right now seems hopeless, with no change in sight. Like the sailor in the crow's nest crying out "Land ahoy," you must keep that vision of safe harbor in your mind's eye and reaffirm hope in your future together with your loved one.

Endnotes

1. William Styron, *Darkness Visible: A Memoir of Madness*, (New York: Random House, 1990).
2. Melody Beattie, *Codependent No More*, (San Francisco: Harper/Hazelden, 1987).

12

Types of Available Treatment

There *is* hope for depression. It can almost always be treated, although at present it is estimated that only one person in five gets help. According to a recent report issued by the National Academy of Sciences' Institute of Medicine, "Despite the availability of new drugs to improve treatment of depression, only a small percentage of elderly people who are depressed are receiving adequate treatment."[1]

Unfortunately treatment for depression is not quite as simple as giving someone a penicillin shot to cure him or her of an infection. Each person's depression comes from a variety of sources previously mentioned—emotional makeup, genetic factors, situational stress, other diseases and disorders, and so on.

In treating depression specialists must determine on an individual basis what will work best with *each particular patient*. This means that the drug used to help your neighbor's mother will not necessarily work with your brother—and, if it does, it would probably require a different dosage. Of necessity this is often a painfully slow process and one that entails much trial and error, as your relative's physician tries to find the ideal match between patient and treatment, between depression and drug tolerance.

Unfortunately each treatment failure only serves to underscore the depressed person's thinking that his or her condition is permanent and that there is no way to ever find relief. Each day that passes first into weeks, and then months, seems a mocking eternity.

Your job as caregiver and family member is to preach patience, even when you yourself feel bereft of it; to offer hope to fill the void of hopelessness; and to gear up yourself, your depressed family member, and the rest of the family so you all can cope with the long days to come.

Begin with a medical checkup

The first step in treating depression always must be a physical examination to rule out other disorders and diseases that may be causing the depression. While it's possible and often the case that someone has another illness in addition to the depression, it's necessary to have this information gained through a complete physical examination in order to treat both disorders.

While some depressions are self-limiting and do go away without treatment, many require one or more forms of treatment. Only your physician can properly advise you; do not try to diagnose or treat your family member yourself. What you all may decide is "only" depression may be such a severe depression that your relative is considering suicide; or it may be depression caused by an underlying additional physical disorder that demands prompt treatment before it becomes more serious.

If the depressed family member is elderly, have one other member of the family stay with him or her for part of the time the doctor is there, to help with questions as well as to observe. Some physicians tend to consider depression in the elderly as normal and conduct examinations of the elderly in a rather perfunctory manner. If the doctor talks only to you rather than the patient, or talks down to the elderly person (calling her "granny" or him "gramps," for instance), find another physician, either a gerontologist (a doctor specializing in older patients) or a more compassionate doctor.

Talk therapy

Probably the best known type of treatment for depression is one of the many forms of psychotherapy, often known collectively as talk therapy. It can take place on a one-to-one basis, in group meetings, or just with the depressed person and other family members meeting with the therapist. Often the entire family or spouse will meet with the therapist early in the treatment, with the depressed person taking part in one-on-one talks with the therapist in the later stages.

Although, according to the *Comprehensive Textbook of Psychiatry (4th ed.)* ". . . family therapy is not generally viewed as a primary therapy for the treatment of depression . . . its use is indicated in cases where (1) an individual's depression appears to be seriously jeopardizing that person's marriage or family functioning or both, or (2) an individual's depression appears to be promoted and maintained by marital or family interaction patterns or both."[2]

Don't be surprised or feel threatened if your loved one's therapist does request that you and other family members come to specific sessions. Answer the therapist's questions honestly and fully. You're all there for the same reason: to help your family member cope and recover from depression. You all may learn some ways to cope, thus making a most difficult and painful time more tolerable.

There are many different types of talk therapy as well. Psychoanalysis is probably the first that comes to mind, with most people conjuring up the image of the patient lying on a couch with the therapist sitting behind, taking notes. This therapy mode often lasts over a period of years, as the patient grapples with problems deep in the unconscious that have been repressed.

Most newer therapies used to treat depression deal in what's called "the here and now." Some, such as Interpersonal Psychotherapy, also known as IPT, are ". . . designed specifically for the needs of depressed patients. It is a focused, short-term, time-limited therapy that emphasizes the current interpersonal relations of the depressed patient while recognizing the role of genetic, biochemical, developmental, and personality factors in causation of and vulnerability to depression."[3] As with many talk therapies, IPT may be used in conjunction with drug therapy.

According to Ellen Frank, Ph.D., associate professor of psychiatry at the University of Pittsburgh, who utilizes IPT in her work, "recent studies using IPT show that this type of therapy not only is effective in getting people out of depression, but that for people with repeated episodes of depression, it may lengthen the wellness interval. This is not to say that IPT can compete with medication, however, but rather that it can be helpful in preventing such frequent recurrences, especially for those who cannot take medication due to other existing medical conditions."

Cognitive therapy is another form of short-term therapy used in treating depression. According to Aaron T. Beck, M.D., author of the Beck Depression Inventory (a questionnaire used by therapists to determine the severity of a depression), and designer of the cognitive therapy mode of treatment, "cognitive therapy can be called the power of *realistic* thinking."[4] It deals with changing the negative way in which a depressed person thinks of him or herself or of a situation. Very simplistically, when a person thinks something is bad, overwhelming, or hopeless, he or she tends to react in response to the way the experience is perceived. In cognitive therapy, the therapist works with the person to realize a more realistic viewpoint.

All talk therapies have a few common characteristics: they help the person learn to express pent-up emotions, discover new and more satisfying ways to cope, and offer within their appointment hour a sanctuary for thoughts, a safe place to discover oneself.

Drug therapy

As many depressions have a chemical basis, drug therapy used alone or in combination with talk therapy can alter the brain's chemistry in such a way that the depression is eased and the person can begin to recover. Unfortunately, as with antibiotics used to treat infections, not everyone responds to a particular antidepressant drug in the same way. Doctors must be careful to prescribe not only the right drug for a specific depression but also the proper dosage. As people assimilate drugs differently, especially children and the elderly, this must of necessity become a delicate process of trial and error.

Unfortunately we are a "quick fix" society. We expect someone to take a magical pill and feel better almost as soon as he or she puts down the glass of water. It doesn't happen this way with antidepressants. It takes time—sometimes from two to six weeks or even more—before the doctor, patient, or family sees any improvement. Often the patient may swear nothing has changed, but the family notices a slight difference. It's important to write any such changes down, as the doctor must rely heavily on reports from both the patient and the family.

Sometimes all this time will pass and there'll be no improvement. Either the drug isn't effective on your family member or the dosage needs to be increased. Meanwhile your loved one is still painfully depressed and, in addition to the depression, is now suffering from one or more side effects from the medication.

All drugs have some side effects. Some have more than others, and some people are more susceptible to drugs than others and have more discomfort from most medications. That's why the physician treating someone with antidepressants needs to be knowledgeable about these drugs and why he or she, along with the patient and the rest of you, have to have patience.

When the doctor prescribes a particular drug for your family member, he or she probably will mention that it has some side effects. If not, ask. You need to understand what the drugs are, what they are supposed to do, when you might see results, what side effects are possible as well as probable, and what you can do to give your relative some relief from the side effects. If the physician tends to dismiss potential problems with a wave and a casual "Oh, the side effects shouldn't be too bad," be concerned. While a few people may have a reaction because they expected to, the majority do better—as we, their family, do—when we all know what to expect.

Antidepressants do have a series of unpleasant side effects including nausea, fatigue, dry mouth, dizziness when standing quickly, constipation, and weight gain that must be dealt with. Fortunately few people have every possible side effect listed for a particular medication, and some have none; but no physician can predict exactly how a particular person will react until the patient actually takes the medication.

Your family member's physician can, however, offer suggestions to make these troublesome side effects more bearable. Sucking sugarless mints or chewing gum can help alleviate a dry mouth, for example. More fiber through extra fruits and vegetables and at least eight eight-ounce glasses of water daily can help reduce problems of constipation. Do not let your family member begin to rely on laxatives, however, unless they are prescribed by the physician. Laxatives can quickly become habit-forming, causing the user to constantly increase the dosage in order to have satisfactory results.

Those who feel fatigued as a result of taking antidepressants can take them at bedtime, to reduce difficulties during waking hours. Wearers of contact lenses may need to switch to eyeglasses during the course of treatment if the antidepressant causes dry eyes.

Be supportive if your depressed relative complains about these or other troublesome side effects. It's human nature to want to stop taking pills if they are making you feel worse than you did before, especially if no one pays any attention to how much worse you really are feeling. Don't let them stop. Use whatever persuasive techniques you know, but don't let them drop the medication in order to "feel better." Drugs can't help the depression if they aren't being taken. Yet many depressed people hide their medication under the bed or flush it down the toilet, because they can't handle the extra burden of the side effects on top of the pain of their depression, while their family waits patiently in vain to see results from the most recent prescription.

Sometimes, after all this waiting and coping with troublesome side effects, the doctor will decide that this particular drug isn't going to be effective or that the side effects are too much for the person to handle just now. Then even more time must pass until the present medication is completely out of the person's system and another can be tried. The waiting seems interminable, not only by the person who's depressed but by his or her family as well.

Try to remember this when well-meaning friends say, "But he's been on the medication for two weeks. Why isn't he better?" or worse, "Why is he still taking the medication? He seems better."

Make sure that your family member *is* still taking the medication properly even though it doesn't seem to be working. Don't either of you give up too soon. A psychiatrist or other physician specializing in treating depression has many drugs available for use. Don't feel all is lost if the first one isn't effective.

Be sure to give the doctor a list of any other medications—prescription and over-the-counter—that your family member is taking and ask if anything is contraindicated while the person is on antidepressants or other medications used in treating depression. Even aspirin, which many of us don't even consider "real" medicine, may cause problems when taken with certain types of antidepressants, tranquilizers, and sleeping pills. Ask about the use of alcohol in combination with medications being used to treat the depression as well. Often the alcohol will heighten the effect of the antidepressant drugs and may create a serious situation. Don't just assume that the physician will mention these cautions to you. They should, of course, but most doctors are tremendously overworked and see many patients in a typical workday. They may think they told you the warnings when in reality it was the family of the patient seen just before. Never assume. Ask.

Anytime your family member is on medication for depression and you think he or she is acting strangely—sleeping too much, vomiting, becoming agitated and hyperactive or sluggish and nonresponsive, contact the doctor immediately. A person who is depressed may not realize how a drug is reacting or be unable to verbalize such changes. You and other family members must become the watchdogs and remain on constant alert.

In addition, whenever a new medication is prescribed for your depressed family member, ask the doctor to list in writing its name, description, and exact dosage. Many pills resemble one another, and if you attribute specific side effects from "the yellow pill" rather than "the yellow capsule," the physician may become confused as to which drug you are discussing. The names of the various medications are just part of the foreign language you must learn while a family member is in the state of depression.

It helps to make a chart to help keep track of each medication and when it needs to be taken. As a depressed person may not remember whether or not he or she actually took the pills, you and other family members may have to take the responsibility for disbursement. It is most important that the correct dosage be taken in order to see if a particular drug is effective.

Watch for overdoses as well. Your family member may take the pills, forget that he or she did, and so take them again. A chart or plastic pill dispenser (available at most pharmacies) may help jog the memory.

You also must urge the depressed person to continue

taking the medication even after he or she begins to feel better. You may meet with some resistance from your loved one who argues that he or she "isn't depressed" anymore. You may hesitate and find it difficult to be convincing. It's human nature for us all to stop taking pills once they begin to be effective, much to the chagrin of our doctors, who want us to take the entire prescribed amount. How many bottles of antibiotics do *you* have in the medicine cabinet with one or two pills left in them?

There is an overwhelming variety of drugs now on the market to help with depression, with new ones about to be introduced. Their names are often long and confusing, and each of them comes with a specific list of possible side effects. They include the major antidepressants, the tricyclics, such as Elavil, Endep, Pamelor, Tofranil, Imavate, and Sinequan, to name a few. Used successfully for many years, these tricyclics have been proven to be effective with depression (although they also can be lethal if taken in an overdose, which is always a possibility when dealing with someone who is depressed). These drugs act by changing the chemical makeup in the brain.

According to the National Institutes of Health, tricyclic antidepressants prevent recurrences in about two-thirds of patients with unipolar depression. There are problems with long-term tricyclic administration—weight gain and, in older people, possible cardiac problems. Nevertheless, if a person has a fairly rapidly recurring depressive illness that represents a major interference with his or her life, then some form of preventive treatment is indicated.[5]

Prozac, the most recent "miracle" drug, is one of what's called "second-generation" antidepressants and at this writing is the most widely prescribed antidepressant in America. Once hoped to be the perfect drug for depression because of its seemingly few side effects, it has garnered some reports that a few, albeit small percent, of patients developed suicidal thoughts while on the drug. The majority of patients on Prozac thus far, however, feel that their depression has lightened with few troublesome side effects.

This only underscores the importance of following your doctor's advice completely when someone is on any type of medication for depression, and of being ever-observant for any changes in behavior. You know your loved one best; you often will be the first to notice subtle alterations in behavior.

Another type of antidepressant, known as the mono-amine oxidase inhibitors, "MAOIs" (Parnate, Nardil, and Marplan, to name a few) also may be effective with specific types of depression, including those that don't respond to other antidepressant drugs. These MAOIs, however, can create dangerous high blood pressure in patients who don't avoid a specific list of foods that includes, among many other items, aged cheeses, wine, beer, avocado, liver, and yogurt. This is only a *partial* listing of prohibited foods for those on monoamine oxidase inhibitors. The physician will furnish a complete list when he or she prescribes the medication. Take the dietary prohibition cautions and other contraindications seriously. Your loved one's well-being depends on it.

There also are tranquilizers used to quell the anxiety that often comes with depression. Bipolar depressions are often treated with good success by a drug known as lithium carbonate. Most experts believe that any patient who has had at least two manic episodes probably should be on lithium maintenance indefinitely unless side effects become more troublesome than the mania.

Shock therapy

Shock therapy, also known as electroconvulsive therapy, or ECT, is coming back into use in recent years after falling out of favor. Although physicians don't know exactly *how* it works, they do know that it does work, especially with those depressed people who have not responded to drugs, cannot take drugs for other existing medical conditions, or who are suicidal.

Most of us wrinkle our noses at the thought of shock therapy and shake our heads violently when it comes to considering ECT for someone we love. The frightening scenes in the late night movies, especially the film *One Flew Over the Cuckoo's Nest*, make ECT seem more like torture than treatment.

While there is still some disagreement among mental health experts concerning the use of ECT, many doctors and patients alike praise its successful effects. Its purpose is to create a seizure in the brain which, for some reason, activates the release of chemicals that in turn reduce depression. The actual procedure itself has undergone some changes since the 40s and 50s.

Before beginning the treatment, patients are given a muscle relaxant injection to prevent muscles from violently contracting during the jolt of current and thereby possibly causing broken bones. In addition, a light anesthesia is used to put the person to sleep and to keep him or her sleeping throughout the entire procedure. Through electrodes attached to one or both sides of the person's head, a small current of electricity is sent through the brain for a second or less, thus creating a type of seizure. While some memory loss does result from the use of ECT, most of it eventually returns.

Many geriatric psychiatrists report good success using electroconvulsive therapy on elderly depressed patients who are less able to tolerate the side effects of antidepressants.

"I fought the idea of my mother having shock treatment," a middle-aged woman told me in a whisper. "It sounded positively barbaric. She was seventy years old. I thought it would kill her. Finally my brothers and sisters convinced me to try it, to see if it would help her. We had tried everything else, and she reacted badly to all the drugs. She had ECT treatment three times a week for three weeks. I couldn't believe the improvement. She smiled and began to take an interest in her appearance. The best part was that *she* didn't seem to mind the treatments. 'After all, I sleep through them,' she said. "I wish we had used it earlier."

ECT also is often used successfully with those considered to be potential suicides when the doctor feels that there is not time to wait for drug therapy to take effect.

Usually doctors call on a combination of treatments in treating depression. According to one study of treatment for depression, "researchers at Brown University have found that patients given cognitive therapy or social skills training in addition to antidepressant drugs are more likely to remit (recover and not relapse) over a one-year period than those who are given only standard drug therapy."[6]

Electroconvulsive therapy, like drugs and talk therapy, is not a permanent cure for depression. For many people, these treatments are successful only in allowing the present depression to lift and having longer periods of "wellness" before the next depression period, thereby permitting the former sufferer to return to work and family, and to enjoy his or her life.

Endnotes

1. Robert L. Berg and Joseph S. Cassells, authors of report for the National Academy of Sciences' Institute of Medicine, 1990.
2. Harold I. Kaplan, M.D., and Benjamin J. Sadock, M.D., eds., *Comprehensive Textbook of Psychiatry* (4th ed.), (Baltimore: Williams & Williams, 1985), p. 819.
3. Gerald L. Klerman, Myrna M. Weissman, Bruce J. Rounsaville, and Eve S. Chevron, *Interpersonal Psychotherapy of Depression*, (New York: Basic Books, 1984).
4. Aaron T. Beck, John A. Rush, Brian F. Shaw, and Gary Emery, *Cognitive Therapy of Depression*, (New York: The Guilford Press, 1979).
5. Office of Clinical Center Communications, National Institutes of Health, Building 10, Room 1C255, Bethesda, MD 20892.
6. Ivan W. Miller, William H. Norman, and Garbor I. Keitner, "Cognitive-behavioral treatment of depressed inpatients: six and

twelve-month follow-up.'' *American Journal of Psychiatry*, 146 (October 1989): p. 1274–1279, as reported in *The Harvard Medical School Mental Health Letter*, Vol. 6, No. 11 (May 1990).

13

What To Do When Someone Talks Of Suicide

Chances are that many readers of this book will never see this chapter. Although they want to learn about and understand depression, they shy away from the "S" word. No, not sex, because Americans, Puritanical beginnings and all, freely sell sex along with blue jeans and soft drinks. Television and movie depictions of sexual intercourse are far more instructional than anything *I* ever learned in 7th grade hygiene class. The only groups not talking about sex are millions of parents and numerous school systems who decline to discuss sex because "it might give the kids ideas."

But if sex talks are taboo in some areas, the real "S" word, "Suicide," is even more widely censored. Euphemisms, like "I'm afraid he might 'do something' to himself," are used instead. Just as the word cancer used to be whispered for fear of catching it, suicide remains in the closet along with goblins and ghosts of our unconscious. If we don't let it out, we reason, it can't get us.

But, sadly, suicide *does* get too many of us. Suicide attempts are increasing worldwide. Suicide destroys not only more than thirty thousand Americans each year—including almost five thousand young people between the ages of fifteen and twenty-four—but like a hurricane it also leaves untold destruction among family and friends in its wake.

183

Unfortunately not everyone who is considering suicide gives us clues. Often the bewildered family says, "but he seemed so happy. Everything was going his way. He was so successful. How could he do it?" or "She was the perfect child. Why would she kill herself?" The survivors struggle with endless feelings of anger, resentment, and guilt. "If only I had known, I could have done something, helped somehow . . ." becomes their agonized mantra. Unknown to them as well, their relative's successful suicide attempt has statistically now placed them in a higher risk category for suicide.

Poet Edwin Arlington Robinson knew that an external show of contentment may only hide internal strife and expressed this knowledge in his powerful work, "Richard Cory." Perhaps you remember it from your high school literature class:

Whenever Richard Cory went down town,
We people on the pavement looked at him:
He was a gentleman from sole to crown,
Clean favored, and imperially slim.

And he was always quietly arrayed,
And he was always human when he talked;
But still he fluttered pulses when he said,
"Good-morning," and he glittered when he walked.

And he was rich—yes, richer than a king—
And admirably schooled in every grace:
In fine, we thought that he was everything
To make us wish that we were in his place.

So on we worked, and waited for the light,
And went without the meat, and cursed the bread;
And Richard Cory, one calm summer night,
Went home and put a bullet through his head.[1]

Many people, however, about three-fourths of those who take their own lives, are unlike the fictional Richard Cory and do leave ample clues for us *if* we are knowledgeable of them and are willing to remain alert for them. This is truly a case where ignorance can be lethal. We don't have to become trained suicidologists to understand how to recognize the clues so often given by someone who is suicidal. All of us—parents, adult children, extended family members, teachers, co-workers, and friends—must be ever-watchful for signs of potential suicide with those who are depressed and always take all suicide threats seriously, understanding as we do so that often suicide cannot be prevented even with our best intentions.

Know the warning signs of suicide

Remember that one of the signs of depression is suicidal thoughts or behavior. Never assume that your depressed loved one is not thinking about suicide just because he or she has never mentioned it. Study this list of warning signs of possible suicide and be ready to act immediately if someone you know is:

Talking about killing him or herself

Do not believe the myth that says, "People who talk about suicide never do it." That's not true. People who talk about killing themselves often DO attempt suicide, and many are successful. Take all suicide threats seriously.

Never deny or belittle someone's threat to kill him or herself. Even if the person changes his or her mind an hour later, the depressive may be serious at the time. Your taunt or denial of his or her feelings might be a trigger to *prove* to you that the threat is serious.

"I got so tired of my wife threatening all the time to kill herself that I finally screamed, 'Fine. Go ahead and do it. Get it over with,' " a man admitted to his wife's psychologist. To his horror, she carried out her threat.

The elderly are also at great risk for potential suicide. According to one study, ". . . suicide occurs at a higher rate among elderly men than among older women . . ."[2] Another states, "The highest suicide rates were found in age groups above 55 years old, rising progressively from 32 per 1,000 in the 50 to 54 age group to 48 per 1,000 in the age group above 74."[3]

Depressed senior citizens may suffer from a myriad of physical disorders that create unending pain and other unpleasant side effects that they're told, "You just have to learn to live with." In despair over bodies and memories that are beginning to fail and seeing no glimmer of hope for their future, suicide often seems the only way out. Rather than becoming helpless emotional, physical, and financial burdens on their adult children, these older depressives, feeling unneeded and unwanted, have both the opportunity and the means to end their lives. Frequently alone for hours or days on end, with few friends left to turn to for comfort, they may overdose on any of anumber of drugs so freely prescribed by any of their many physicians, or plow their cars into trees (reported as "single car accidents"), shoot themselves with guns left for self-protection by well-meaning adult children, or otherwise end their lives. Their children and grandchildren compare notes and find that "Grandma said she didn't want to be a burden, but I didn't think she *meant* anything by it," or "Dad said he'd never go to a nursing home; he'd rather die first, but I never took him seriously."

Heed these cries for help. Do not turn your back on someone you think may be suicidal; have a relative or friend stay with them until you can arrange for professional help. In their hopeless and forlorn state, potential suicides feel too much pain to see any other way out; YOU must gently offer support and guide them out of their bleak shadows.

Acting out self-destructive behavior

Many depressed people behave in a reckless way—driving too fast, jumping from high places, playing with guns, dodging into traffic, mixing alcohol with drugs, committing petty crimes, engaging in promiscuous sex or, in youngsters, running away from home—as they tempt fate. Their depression makes them feel helpless and hopeless so they act as though they don't care if they live or die.

"I really couldn't bring myself to slash my wrists or shoot myself," a teenager said, speaking quite unemotionally to me about his past bouts of depression, "so I'd race the car as fast as it would go. I'd get it up to ninety miles an hour, figuring that if I flipped or missed a turn, good riddance. I wouldn't feel such pain anymore, and it wouldn't be my fault. That way it wouldn't hurt my folks as much."

Many so-called fatal accidents are actually successful suicide attempts. Physicians may cite "confusion over dosage" to protect families from the stigma of someone in the family trying or succeeding in a suicide attempt. Yet most people who attempt suicide really don't want to kill themselves. They simply want to stop hurting. Their attempts are a cry for help.

The trigger for a suicide attempt by many teenagers is getting into trouble either at school or with the police and being afraid of what might happen. "I couldn't face my parents," said one teen who attempted suicide by turning the family's car motor on in a closed garage, only to be rescued by her parents. "I was so humiliated. I preferred death to seeing their hurt faces."

Giving away favorite possessions

Someone who is suicidal may give away a cherished item to a friend or sibling, saying, "Here, I won't be needing this anymore," or "I'd like you to look after my dog if anything happens to me." A person may suddenly make out a will or otherwise "tidy up" his or her affairs.

Increasing use of drugs and alcohol

Alcohol and many drugs are depressants and, rather than bolstering a depressed person's low self-image, these chemicals actually serve to make someone feel even more depressed. They also tend to loosen inhibitions, making someone who is considering suicide more likely to attempt it.

A depressive being treated with antidepressants may mix the drugs with alcohol as an attempt at suicide or drive under the influence of alcohol hoping to "end it all" in an automobile accident. Unfortunately this latter situation often ends even more tragically, as the driver slams into other cars, often killing entire families at one time. If the depressive survives the crash, he or she then must cope with not only the guilt but also the legal problems that follow.

Withdrawing from family, friends, and former activities

Depressed people, in general, tend to withdraw. It is their way of giving up, of allowing the passivity of depression to wash over them. For someone who is suicidal it is also an unconscious way of pulling away, creating distance between him or herself and friends and family members in preparation for death.

According to many studies, the suicide rate for single adults living alone is higher than for their married counterparts.[4] Perhaps it's because a single person who lives alone can easily become isolated without others noticing for some time, much as with the elderly person who may live alone or with an elderly mate who is in poor physical or emotional health and thus is in no condition to become aware of the spouse's growing depression and isolation.

Changing behaviors suddenly

A person who has been in a depression and suddenly seems upbeat and frantic with activity may not be better at all but rather may have decided to attempt suicide and is just "tying up loose ends." Someone who formerly was meticulous about his or her appearance may go without bathing or changing clothes. A good worker or student may suddenly show little interest in achievement. Someone with normal eating habits may begin to start binging or become anorexic and/or bulimic. Acknowledge this sudden behavioral change by saying something like, "You seem different lately. You don't seem to care about your work anymore," or "you seem to have lost interest in your appearance," or "I've never seen you seem so busy. What's going on?" Try to make it easy for the depressed person to confide in you. Don't be afraid to ask questions or to show you care.

Identifying with someone who has committed suicide

Recently there has been a great deal of concern about so-called "copycat suicides," in which people, primarily but not only youngsters, attempt to commit suicide shortly after someone they know has killed themselves or after seeing a movie or television show about suicide. They may see suicide in a romantic way, as in *Romeo and Juliet* or after reading about Marilyn Monroe or author Sylvia Plath.

Adolescents who are struggling with low self-images and a sense of isolation and despair may see suicide as a way to receive recognition from peers and the media, without understanding or acknowledging the finality of such an act.

If you have school-age children, be sure your school system is prepared with an emergency plan to spring into action if a youngster does commit suicide. Classmates and close friends will be in need of counseling, and high-risk youngsters should be assessed and given particular care to prevent "cluster suicides." Teachers should be trained to facilitate discussion in their classrooms to help youngsters express their feelings. PTA and other parent organizations should also be educated in ways to help their children deal with a suicide among their peers. Pretending it didn't happen will only drive emotions underground, not make them go away. According to experts, there is "evidence that exposure to a suicide that was not part of a cluster may lead certain persons to take their own lives."[5]

Unfortunately lack of funding often prevents school systems from having full-time counselors who are trained in suicide prevention. "My school gets a visit from the psychologist once a week for half a day," a junior high teacher said. "What am I supposed to say to a high-risk youngster who may jump out of the window at any time? 'Wait until next Thursday'?"

Be especially cautious if someone in the family previously committed or attempted to commit suicide. New studies just released at this writing suggest ways in the near future to uncover genetic markers in order to discover those who may be more vulnerable to suicide attempts. In addition to genetic factors, however, there is also the modeling factor, through which other family members may have unconsciously accepted that pattern of coping with stress and disappointment. A previous suicide attempt raises the likelihood that the depressed person will try suicide again. According to various studies, anywhere between 35 and 60 percent of those who kill themselves have had at least one prior attempt.

"Oh, well, I can always kill myself," a friend once said to me after being laid off from her job, speaking half in jest and half in truth. We began talking about her brother, who had killed himself by parking his car on the train tracks and waiting for the train to come to end his pain. When she realized that she had always considered suicide a way out for her as well if things got too bad, she was surprised. Fortunately her story thus far has been happier. Realizing her vulnerability to a possible suicide attempt, she arranged for counseling and has been able to develop healthier ways of coping.

Some people may react to a loved one's death by wanting to "jump on the funeral pyre." Overwhelmed by grief and depression, they may decide that life really isn't worth living without the one they love and in their depression see no other alternatives; so they begin to make plans to join him or her in death.

Never be afraid that asking someone if he or she is thinking about suicide will give him or her ideas. Actually someone who is thinking about suicide already has the ideas and may be relieved to share these frightening feelings.

Listen and try to remain calm. Don't say, "Oh that's silly," or "You must be crazy to think that." Instead ask for more information by saying, "Do you think you'd be better off dead?" or "Are you planning to hurt yourself?" "Have you planned how?" If the answer to any of these questions is yes, seek immediate professional help.

"You cannot keep a suicidal intent confidential," warns Dr. Sol Gordon in his book *When Living Hurts*. He adds, "In some cases you may find yourself in the position of having to get direct help for someone who is suicidal and refuses to go for counseling. If so, do it. Don't be afraid of appearing disloyal. Many people who are suicidal have given up hope. They no longer believe they can be helped. They feel it is useless. The truth is, they *can* be helped. . . . What at the time may appear to be an act of disloyalty or the breaking of a confidence could turn out to be the favor of a lifetime. Your courage and willingness to act could save a life."[6]

Treating potential suicides is *not* a job for amateurs, even those who care about the depressed person a great deal. You may think you've talked your family member out of suicide when all he or she is doing is clamming up and keeping all the feelings inside until they explode with horrifying results.

Don't assume you can relax your vigil once your relative seems to be getting better either. Strangely enough, many depressives attempt suicide once they do begin to recover. Experts say it is because in the depths of depression, the sufferer may be too passive and overwhelmed to take any type of action. Once the depression lifts a bit, however, the pain is still there, and the person has a higher energy level to try to take his or her life. According to Dr. Gerald L. Klerman of Cornell University Medical Center, ''Death by suicide occurs at the rate of about 1 percent during the year of the acute episode and 15 percent over the lifetime of a patient with recurrent depressions . . . the highest suicide mortality occurs during the six-to-nine month period after symptomatic improvement has occurred.[7]

Always contact a crisis center or medical help immediately if you fear someone is suicidal and do not leave them alone. You may have to agree to hospitalization for them, but you could be saving your depressed family member's life.

Children *do* commit suicide

Never assume that a child is too young to attempt suicide. According to the National Center for Health Statistics, ''In 1984 there were 7 reported suicides in children aged 5 to 9 years and 225 suicides in those aged 10 to 14 years in the United States.''[8] Sadly, according to experts, suicide rates are increasing considerably in children under the age of ten. Theories as to why this is happening vary but include the increasing stresses our society inflicts on youngsters; biological influences or chemical imbalances in the brain; loss of self-worth in today's world; and the ''romanticizing of suicide'' in movies, TV, and literature that influences the immature child, who doesn't realize that death is permanent.

The following list of ways in which parents can reduce the risk of depression and suicide in their children is adapted from a booklet published by the William Gladden Foundation, entitled "Children, Depression and Suicide."[9] It includes:

> Finding ways to help your child develop and maintain a positive self-image.

Be sure that neither you nor your child have nonrealistic expectations. I vividly remember one year with little league when my son's coach had such high expectations for *his* son that the rest of us parents cringed at every game. While the coach was supportive of our sons, he drove his son—a nonathlete—to excel in baseball. This hapless youngster stood near second base, moving seconds too late to catch fly balls and scooping up dust with his mitt as the baseball rolled between his legs and into the outfield. His father yelled and cursed, trying to make his son into the baseball player the father had always wanted to be. Eventually we parents demanded the father's resignation as coach. Too bad we couldn't have demanded his resignation as father as well. We lost touch with the youngster but often wondered how his father's unrealistic desires had affected that child's self-image.

Many youngsters who attempt suicide do so because they feel they have failed to live up to their parents' or their own expectations. Each spring the grapevine trembles with the news of some high school senior who wasn't accepted by the "right" school and decided life was over; in fall, it's when football cuts are made, and sons of former football greats don't make the team. Unable to handle the disappointment and ensuing sense of failure, or feeling that they won't be accepted and loved by their parents because they have not lived up to parental expectations, these young people choose to escape by taking their own lives.

To a youngster who's already depressed, these and other failures often are the final sign confirming what they already knew: that they are worthless, unwanted, and have "no right to live."

> Teaching and encouraging your child to
> communicate openly in order to reduce feelings
> of being "trapped."

Many children find no one home—physically or emotionally—when they need to talk. Others may have picked up cues concerning what may and may not be discussed in their home. Rather than upsetting the family equilibrium by talking about their depression and frustration, they keep their feelings to themselves, allowing them to smolder, needing only time before they burst into flames.

Experts estimate that about 20 percent of youngsters who attempt suicide have one or both parents who suffer from drinking problems, which also may contribute to difficulties with communication skills. Young people with parents who are depressed also are at a high risk for suicide.

> Teaching your child that stress is part of life,
> along with "healthy" ways to handle it.

As with many parenting skills, teaching your child how to handle stress and disappointments most effectively comes from what you *do*, not what you *say*. If you have difficulty or aren't satisfied with how you handle stress and frustrations, admit it to your youngster and begin to work as a family to improve these techniques.

As my grandmother once said, "Everyone has something. Nobody gets out of this life untouched"; so you might as well learn now how to cope with disappointment when things don't go your way. Youngsters who don't learn these skills while they're still at home may be devastated when they receive their first "D" at college or aren't selected by the fraternity or sorority of their choice and have no parents on hand to help cushion the blow.

> Allowing your child to help make personal and
> family decisions in order to feel "empowered"
> and responsible.

Feelings of uselessness and helplessness add to a person's depression. Without overwhelming a youngster with decisions too monumental for him or her to handle (such as "Should I leave your father?" or "Do you think Joe and I should get married?"), create opportunities for a young person to become comfortable with decision-making skills and to learn to live with the results of these decisions.

Rather than telling a disgruntled youngster to quit the basketball team because he's stuck on the bench, for example, ask questions to help him make his own decision. "Do you enjoy practices enough to compensate for not playing in the actual games?" "Do you enjoy the camaraderie that being on the team provides?" "What would you do for exercise or with your time if you weren't out for basketball?" He may decide either to quit or stick it out. The decision itself isn't as important as the making of it. It puts the young person in charge of his or her life, and that builds a good self-image.

It's often hard to keep your mouth shut when the obvious decision seems, well, so obvious. But it's important to let your youngster go through the decision-making process. Offer food for thought, but let your child do the chewing. Sometimes the best parenting skill is to keep still. If your young person asks for your opinion, give it, but also give quiet assurance that you have confidence in his or her judgment.

> Developing and maintaining a stable home
> environment.

While ideally every child would come from a loving and intact two-parent home, this obviously isn't always the case. Some youngsters have lost one or both parents through death, some through divorce. In many two-parent homes, however, the dysfunctional aspects of drug addiciton and alcoholism, poor parenting skills, lack of communication skills, and parents' depression, far outweigh any supposed benefit of having two parents. Rather than nurturing, the home environment poisons, and the sense of isolation and hopelessness fostered there triggers depression and hopelessness and seemingly offers no other way out for the troubled youngster than suicide. No wonder that statistics reveal that almost 65 percent of those children attempting (but failing) to commit suicide come from broken and dysfunctional homes.

There's no doubt that it's often more difficult to provide a stable home environment when you have to be both mother and father plus, often, the entire extended family; yet thousands of single parents have proven that it can be done. But you need to accept help from others—schools, coaches, churches and synagogues, relatives, Big Brother/Big Sister programs, and other community services.

Becoming aware that you need the help is the first step; accepting it is the second. Your child's well-being depends on it. Never try to do it all yourself. Parenting is too important a job to attempt alone. Accept the help that your community offers and then reach out to others to show *them* how it can be done. It goes back to what Dr. Sol Gordon calls the "each one reach one" concept.

> Devoting time and attention to each child so
> that he or she feels special.

Most of us are so busy trying to make a living and cope with life's daily aggravations—the repair person doesn't show up the day we stayed home waiting or the car broke down before we drove it out of the car lot or the boss gave us a report and we had to work late and that was the night we had theatre tickets—that we often take other family members for granted. When you have more than one child, it takes time to give them all a special moment. Too often attention is focused on the "lame duck," one who has a chronic illness, a learning problem, and so on; we tend to let the well ones fend for themselves. It's a mistake, of course, and even more so when someone, especially a child, is depressed. What is needed most at that particular moment is validation of self-worth, because the depressive doesn't feel like much. If we forget to give that special hug or favorable comment, it can build up as reinforcement: "You see, I was right. Even my mother doesn't care."

That's when you can use a helping hand from extended family members, friends, coaches, and others who can help you focus on all your children. Think about it: Was there one person in your life—a teacher, coach, or favored aunt—who made you feel special when you were young? Why? Was it what they said or the fact that they made it obvious that they liked and accepted you just as you were?

It's difficult to ferret out quality time for each child when you're trying to hold down a job (or two jobs), care for the house, possibly look after aging parents, and handle all your other responsibilities. If you have another child who is chronically ill, your other children may suffer from lack of attention. Your depressed child may become the family scapegoat, with all the family's problems being blamed on him or her. It may feed into that child's depression and start him or her thinking, "If I wasn't here, everybody would be happy," or "If I died, they couldn't blame me."

When my five children were small, my husband and I worked very hard to focus on each as individuals rather than on them all as a group. He'd take one to the office on Saturday to go through the mail and have a little father-daughter or father-son talk. I took each on mother-child shopping sprees, sometimes only to the grocery or cleaners, but it allowed some time alone.

Cleaning up after dinner was done on a rotation schedule, partly to spread the responsibilities (ours was an equal opportunity household) and partly to assure time alone with that particular child. We had (and still have) family vacations where we all traveled together, with the change of scene offering good one-on-one occasions long with many memory-making possibilities. It's hard for anyone to feel left out when you're getting soaked while white-water rafting or viewing Niagara Falls on *The Maid of the Mist*. Eating fresh trout you caught just moments before or hiking up a mountain path to look *down* on the clouds are experiences that forever bond individuals into a family joined by common memories. So are holding a garage sale and donating the profits to a favorite charity or joining with others to repair and paint houses for the elderly.

These holidays from our usual school or work pressures, when we worked and played together, paved the way for inside jokes, family stories, and shared memories that become the fabric of a family, weaving individuals into one support system that upholds each when times get hard, as they do in every family.

Each of these vacations and nontraditional activities offered us unpressured time to focus on each youngster, to praise skills we hadn't known they possessed and, even more importantly, to show them where *we* lacked abilities or confidences that they had. When children observe their parents being content with their achievements even though lacking perfection (and sometimes looking downright awkward or silly), it eases the load for the youngsters as well.

Being aware of sudden or dramatic emotional or behavioral changes in your child.

Most of us know our children fairly well. While we probably won't let others criticize them, we could describe them accurately. That's why you may be the first to notice any sudden change in the way your youngster reacts or behaves. A passive child may begin to pick fights; an active youngster may become apathetic. Suddenly your child may become "accident prone," getting unexplained bruises, burns, or cuts.

Your child's teacher also may pick up on a sudden change in your child's behavior, sometimes even before you do. Before you jump to your youngster's defense, listen objectively. He or she may have spotted a major shift in behavior that could signify depression and suicidal tendencies.

A youngster who suddenly loses his or her previous interest in academic achievement, one who shows a fascination with death and dying, or who demonstrates through essays or pictures a preoccupation with death, may be harboring suicidal thoughts. Rather than criticizing the teacher for an overactive imagination, thank him or her for caring and being so attentive. Then get immediate proper professional help for your child.

Don't minimize your young person's sense of loss when a best friend moves away, when love is unrequited, or when a friend, relative, or even a beloved pet dies. Young emotions are painfully raw because they have so little experience to temper them. Kids don't know that, hopefully, many loves will come and go in a lifetime, that losing a class election may have positive aspects in that other opportunities become available, or that one can stay home the night of the homecoming dance and not be marked for life.

But youth is vulnerable, and you need to be aware of how losses and disappointments affect your youngster. The peer group and peer opinion is terribly important to a young person. A sense of rejection and abandonment by the peer group can drive a youngster who lacks self-confidence to attempt suicide as a way to escape what he or she considers "total isolation."

If you feel that your child has trouble relating to his or her peers, try to open discussion gently. Share memories of your youth and how you handled similar problems. If you have difficulty with communication, consider professional talk therapy, as your youngster may find it easier to discuss personal problems first with an objective professional.

A large majority of young people who attempt suicide do feel socially isolated, as though no one really cares if they live or die. Whereas peers may pick up on a friend's depression and thoughts of suicide and possibly be able to head off disaster, the loner is at great risk, because there's often no one to talk to or to talk him or her out of a suicide attempt. A youngster who has few friends or who suddenly has withdrawn from former friends may be sending out a desperate message. Be receptive.

> Knowing each child's friends and their
> behaviors, as children often react to
> their peer group.

According to child psychiatrist Joseph Lupo, depressed people often seek each other out. This is often true with young people who, in searching for a group, any group, may stumble into "the wrong crowd." This is especially prevalent with adolescents who have moved around a great deal and have left former attachments with peers behind. "This is a moving society," said Dr. Lupo. "Some people move an average of every four years. For youngsters, this means not only abandoning friends but also leaving behind starting positions on athletic teams and leadership roles in other school activities, functions that gave them confidence and a good feeling about themselves and their abilities."

Anxious to make friends quickly, a newly transplanted youngster may get into a crowd that uses drugs or alcohol, promotes reckless driving and games of "chicken," is sexually promiscuous, or follows other self-destructive activities. Many experts agree that over half the young people who commit suicide are substance abusers. The drugs and/or alcohol lower inhibitions, making it easier to engage in dangerous activity or to try to "end it all."

Ask about your youngster's friends. Make your home the gathering spot for the gang, so you can see firsthand what they're like. Try to meet their parents, too. Don't worry if they're not like you. What's important is that you share the same values. If you sense that your young person's adopted crowd is negative and anti-everything, try to open communication about it. Ask your young person what he or she likes about the group. Remain ever-watchful for possible self-destructive behavior.

Setting a good example on how you handle stress and disappointments.

There's an old saying: What you *do* speaks so loudly that I can't hear what you *say*. That's the case when you're dealing with your children and why it is so important that you be aware of your silent messages.

How do *you* handle disappointments? Do you catch yourself saying "I could kill myself for being so stupid?" or "I didn't get that promotion. I wish I were dead." You may not have meant it, but the words may have sunk into your child's subconscious.

Discuss in family get-togethers healthy ways in which to handle stress—such as exercise, volunteerism, and relaxation. Most importantly don't keep disappointments and failures to yourself but rather share them with your youngsters, so they grow to learn how to handle them and to accept that failures are not negative reflections on you as a person but rather demonstrate simply that something you tried did not succeed.

Keeping alcohol, drugs, medications, guns, knives, and other potentially dangerous objects locked away from your child, as suicide attempts often are an impulsive response to depression or disappointment.

Most people who attempt suicide want to end their pain, but they really aren't sure they want to die. An unsuccessful attempt may be a cry for someone to help; a successful attempt may be one that no one was around to stop in time. Recognize the warning signs and remove obvious potential weapons whenever possible. According to Dr. Leon Eisenberg, "The impulse to suicide among adolescents commonly waxes and wanes. If opportunity and means for suicide are not at hand, young persons survive the critical period and their spirits usually spring back.''[10]

Often suicide attempts are made during what experts call ''a disciplinary crisis.'' The youngster gets into some type of mischief or difficulty and is so afraid to face the consequences that he or she figures ''I'd be better off dead.'' If the attempt is thwarted, these same adolescents usually are amazed to discover that their parent's wrath or the disciplinary action received was far less traumatic than they had anticipated.

> Helping your child—especially one under twelve—to realize that death is permanent.

The concept of the finality of death is difficult for young children to understand. They may only think ''I'll kill myself and you'll be sorry'' when they're angry or frustrated.

> Seeking professional help if your child seems depressed.

While every depressed person isn't a potential suicide, most people who attempt suicide are depressed. Therefore you need to bring in professional help to deal with the threat of possible suicide.

While you cannot completely suicide-proof your home, you can help reduce the number of weapons of choice. Throw out unused medications and lock up all drugs— both prescription and over-the-counter. If you own guns, give them to friends to lock up in their homes. A depressed person can become very observant when watching for the location of the key to the gun rack.

Some experts feel that the increasing availability of guns in American homes has favored impulsive acts of self-destruction.[11] According to Peter Reich, M.D., of the Massachusetts Institute of Technology, ''The incidence of suicide by firearms has risen from 44.8 percent of all suicides in 1954 to 58.5 percent in 1984, while the rates of suicide by other common methods . . . have remained stable over these years.''[12] "In 1984 guns were used in almost one-half the suicides of 10- to 14-year-olds and nearly 60% of suicides among 15- to 19-year-olds.''[13]

Conversely "in Great Britain, for instance, where possession of firearms without a permit is illegal, suicides with guns are uncommon.''[14] Without taking sides on the gun control controversy, I think it's safe to say that if there is someone who is depressed in your home, suicide is always a possibility, which means there's no place for a gun, too.

Use care also in storing razor blades, knives, and other sharp objects, as well as household poisons such as cleaning fluids, turpentines, and photographic developing liquids.

Keep communication lines open so your family member feels comfortable talking with you. While you can't talk people out of attempting suicide if they've absolutely made up their mind, most people are somewhat ambivalent. They really want to be talked out of killing themselves; they just don't see any other way out. Tell them you care, that you are there for them, and that you won't be shocked if they confide in you just how they feel. Listen. Let them know that you will get them professional help to ease their pain.

More than two hundred communities have suicide prevention centers and twenty-four-hour crisis hot lines where someone may call if they feel they are suicidal. If your area does have such a service, write the telephone number down and place it by every telephone. If you're not present when the urge to attempt suicide comes over your family member, he or she may call that number and speak with a specially trained volunteer who knows how to listen and what to say until help arrives. If your community doesn't offer such a service, begin to establish one.

In addition there are community mental health agencies, trained members of the clergy, private therapists, physicians, school and college counselors, and psychological social workers who are trained to give emotional support to people who feel suicidal. Check your local Yellow Pages or contact your local hospital to learn what's available in your community. The next chapter lists a number of sources of help.

Share that information with your depressed loved one. They need to know that, despite what they are feeling, they are not alone, that people do care about them, and that they can get help to ease their pain. Trust your instinct. If you're concerned that a loved one might "do something," act on that gut feeling and get help now.

Endnotes

1. Edwin Arlington Robinson, "Richard Cory," from his collection, *The Children of the Night*, (New York: Chas. Scribner's Sons, 1897).

2. B. Gurland and P. Cross, "Epidemiology of psychopathology in old age: Some implications for clinical services," *Psychiatr. Clin. North Am.* 5 (1982):11–26. Quoted in "The Diagnosis of Depression in the Elderly," by Thomas A. Ban and Michael H. Ebert, *Affective Disorders*, Frederic Flach, ed. (New York: W.W. Norton & Company, 1988).

3. J. Sendbuehler and S. Goldstein, "Attempted suicide among the aged," *Journal of American Geriatric Society* 25 (1977):245–248. Quoted in "The Diagnosis of Depression in the Elderly," by Thomas A. Ban and Michael H. Ebert, *Affective Disorders*, Frederic Flach, ed. (New York: W.W. Norton & Company, 1988).

4. B.M. Barraclough, J. Bunch, B. Nelson, and P. Sainsbury, "One Hundred Cases of Suicide," *Brit. J. Psychiat.* 125 (1974):355–373.

5. D.P. Phillips and L.L. Carstensen, "Clustering of teenage suicides after television news stories about suicide," *New England Journal of Medicine* 315 (1986):685–9; and M.S. Gould and D. Shaffer, "The impact of suicide in television movies: evidence of imitation," *New England Journal of Medicine* 315 (1986):690–4.

6. Sol Gordon, Ph.D., *When Living Hurts*, (New York: Dell Publishing, 1988). Excerpted from A. Russell Lee and Charlotte P. Ross, *Suicide in Youth and What You Can Do About It*, prepared by the

Suicide Prevention and Crisis Center of San Mateo County, California, in cooperation with the American Association of Suicidology and Merck Sharp & Dohme.

7. Gerald L. Klerman, Myrna M. Weissman, Bruce J. Rounsaville, and Eve S. Chevron, *Interpersonal Psychotherapy of Depression*, (New York: Basic Books, 1984).

8. Kailie R. Shaw, M.D., Kathy H. Sheeham, Ph.D., and Robert C. Fernandez, M.D., "Suicide in Children and Adolescents," Year Book Medical Publishers, Inc., *Adv. Pediatrics* 34:313-334

9. Walnk Brown, *Children, Depression and Suicide*, (York, PA: Gladden Press, 1987).

10. Leon Eisenberg, M.D., editorial in the *New England Journal of Medicine*, September 11, 1986.

11. R.V. Clarke and P.R. Jones, "Suicide and the increased availability of handguns in the United States," *Soc. Sci. Med.*, 28 (1989): 805-9.

12. Peter Reich, M.D., "Panic Attacks and the Risk of Suicide," *New England Journal of Medicine*, Vol. 321, No. 18, 1260-1261.

13. National Center for Health Statistics "Vital Statistics of the U.S. Vol. 2 Part A Hyattsville, Maryland

14. Florence L. Denmark and Ronna M. Kabatznick, "Women and Suicide," in *Affective Disorders*, ed. Frederic Flach (New York: W.W. Norton & Company, 1988).

14

Where To Find Help

If you remember nothing else from this book, remember that you do not need to deal with your loved one's depression all by yourself. There's no shame in having a depressed family member, so don't feel as though you have to keep "the problem" a deep family secret. You may think that you're protecting the ill person, but instead you prevent him or her from getting important support from others, and you also pile unnecessary pressures onto yourself and the other family members. Fortunately there are many—friends, extended family, and community, state, and national organizations already in place to share some of your burden and to offer suggestions to make your load more bearable. Please look this list over and select those that can be of help.

Your family physician

Your family doctor should be your first phone call when you're concerned about a loved one's depression. A complete physical examination is always warranted to rule out possible medical conditions that could be the underlying cause of the depression.

Psychiatrist, psychologist, specially trained social worker

Any of these and other members of your community's social service agencies trained in mental health can be of help dealing with both the depressive and the rest of the family. You can get names by contacting your area's American Psychiatric Association, your community mental health association, the local medical society, or a university or medical school's psychology or psychiatry department. Don't hesitate to ask for qualifications or get recommendations from other knowledgeable health professionals.

Of the above specialties, only psychiatrists are medical doctors able to prescribe medications as well as being trained in emotional and mental health. If the depressed person meets with a nonmedical therapist, he or she will work in consultation with a physician who is trained in the use of drugs.

Members of the clergy

Often one or more members of a family—including the depressive—can be counseled by a member of the clergy if he or she has received proper training in dealing with depression. There already is a certain amount of preexisting trust established in such a situation, and although a nonmedical person cannot prescribe drug therapy, it can be an important beginning for talk therapy.

Your religious leader also can help to ease the burden of guilt you may be feeling and help you to understand that the act of caring for yourself as well as the depressed person is not a selfish one, but instead one that makes rather good sense.

"I felt everyone was judging me," a young woman said. "No matter what I tried to do, I could not make my mother or sister feel good. They both were in depressions, and I was rapidly becoming depressed myself over what I perceived as my failure to make them happy. Thank goodness I talked with my rabbi, who gave me 'permission' to be happy and to spend some time doing those things that made *me* feel good."

Suicide Crisis Center

There are over two hundred suicide crisis centers in the United States alone. The volunteers manning the phones have been especially trained to establish immediate rapport with the distressed caller. In addition to helping to avert a potential suicide, these dedicated workers are knowledgeable about the various helping agencies in your specific community and are able to help guide the caller to one that can be of most help. Look in your telephone book for the number and place it by all your telephone extensions.

National Depressive & Manic-Depression Association
        Box 3395
        Chicago, IL 60654
        (312) 939-2442

This national organization offers excellent printed material and audio tapes for families and sufferers of depression and manic-depression. They also have a newsletter and can send you a list of established support groups near you. There is a charge for many of their books and tapes. Write for their catalogue.

American Psychiatric Association
        Division of Public Affairs
        1400 K. St., N.W.
        Department SG
        Washington, D.C. 20005

This national professional association publishes, along with their professional material, many excellent pamphlets on a number of mental health subjects slanted to lay readership. Although these are sold in bulk rates of fifty, you can request a free sample by writing to the above address and enclosing a stamped, self-addressed, business-size envelope. Be sure to mention which titles you want. A partial listing of their "Let's Talk Facts About . . ." pamphlet series includes the following subjects:

Depression
Teen Suicide
Manic-Depressive Disorder
Substance Abuse
Mental Illness
Mental Health of the Elderly
Choosing a Psychiatrist

American Association of Suicidology
2459 South Ash Street
Denver, CO 80222

This organization offers a variety of printed suicide prevention materials including some specifically slanted to students and teachers. They also offer guidance to schools interested in developing suicide prevention programs.

Depression After Delivery
P.O. Box 1282
Morrisville, PA 19067
(215) 295-3994

This is a lay group offering printed information to help those suffering from postnatal depression. They also can give you a list of women in both the United States and Canada who have suffered from PPD, as well as support groups in your area.

Al-Anon
This is a national support group for families and friends of alcoholics. While they don't focus on depression as such, they do stress positive thinking and AA's Twelve Steps, which many co-dependents find

helpful. If your depressed family member is also an alcoholic, you might consider attending Al-Anon meetings, available in most communities. Look in your local phone book under either Al-Anon or Alcoholics Anonymous.

> Well Spouse Support Groups
>   The Well Spouse Foundation
>   P.O Box 28876
>   San Diego, CA 92128

These groups are springing up throughout the country as a reaction to an excellent book for the well spouse or family member, *Mainstay* by Maggie Strong. In addition to offering help to those who want to establish Well Spouse Support Groups in their communities, this organization publishes a quarterly newsletter. Write to The Well Spouse Foundation at the above address.

> Camp Fire Boys & Girls
>   Dept P
>   4601 Madison Avenue
>   Kansas City, MO 64112

This is a well-known youth organization with its beginnings dating back to 1910. Write to them at the above address and ask for their booklet, "Suicide Awareness: A Teen's Guide to Action."

> Depressives Anonymous
>   329 East 62nd St.
>   New York, NY 10021

This is a support group for those suffering from depression.

Family Services Agencies

Most states offer counseling and other psychotherapeutic services through accredited members of the Family Services Association of America. Your local library or telephone book can give you the name of the Family Service Agency in your community. Unfortunately there is no uniformity of name nationwide, so you may have to look under many classifications, including "Family Services," "Mental Health Services," "Counseling," or "Respite Care." Some religious affiliations have their own family service groups, so contact an appropriate member of the clergy.

Local hospital or mental health associations

These institutions differ from community to community and may offer varying services. Most, however, do have departments that can be of help to families of depressives. Some may even sponsor support groups for such families.

Local or national chapters of organizations dealing with other medical or psychological disorders

Depression often doesn't hit in isolation but rather is part of or co-exists with other disorders. You may find strong family support groups already in existence with your local chapters of the American Heart Association, the American Cancer Society, or in organizations for family members dealing with stroke rehabilitation, Alzheimer's disease, chronic pain, diabetes, blindness or the partially sighted, Tourette syndrome, ileitis and Crohn's disease, MS, and a myriad of other afflictions.

All of these disorders have a depressive component, and you may find comfort and good advice from other family members attending these meetings. It is not a sign of weakness to want this type of support. It just makes good sense. It's an easy way to share information about the disorder and how depression is a part of it, learn new ways of coping with the exhausting problem of dealing with a depressed family member, as well as discovering services that you didn't know existed. It's also a way of meeting new people at a time when your own world may have become very isolated.

If you need a service that isn't being filled, don't keep it to yourself, but share it with others. The more people who know what type of help you need, the more likely you are to find someone who knows someone who had the same problem and may have found a solution.

If you're a caregiver to someone who you fear is suicidal and you're afraid to leave him or her alone, plan today to strengthen your support system. Ask friends to come in to relieve you. There also are adult day-care facilities and short-term nursing agencies and facilities in many communities to provide such ''sitting'' services, known as ''respite care.''

Always have a backup plan for emergencies. You may become ill or want to take a trip. Don't wait until these situations arise. Instead follow the Boy Scout code and ''Be Prepared.''

There is a tangled web of community agencies throughout the United States, and many of them overlap. You may have to spend some time on the telephone until you find exactly what you are looking for. Your local librarian also might be able to offer suggestions if you don't know where to look or what number to call. These dedicated men and women are skilled at retrieving information and often know exactly which reference book to pull off the shelf. Chances are it is far from dusty.

Epilogue

Living with someone who is depressed is a little like falling asleep during a lecture. You know you should fight against it, but the sensation is overwhelming, and it's just easier to give in.

But you must continue to fight against taking on your loved one's depression. Become informed instead. Learn as much as you can about what depression really is, how it can overcome you, and what to look for. Prepare yourself. Once you know the enemy and its disguises, you can begin to do battle with it.

Then you are armed to help your relative in his or her battle against depression. Like a visitor to a foreign land, you'll speak the language and know where it's safe to travel.

Remember that, despite how it may seem right now, most depressions do end. As subtly as they came, they will first lighten, and then leave. Like the beachcomber after the hurricane, you'll find things changed somewhat, but the memory of your night of terror will soon begin to fade a little.

Don't get discouraged; take care of yourself; make time in your life for laughter. I hope that this book has helped in some way for you to begin to see a break in the clouds and look for the rainbow.

Suggested Reading

Herbert Benson, M.D., with Miriam Klipper *The Relaxation Response* (New York: Avon Books, 1975).

Hilde Bruch, M.D. *Golden Cage: The Enigma of Anorexia Nervosa* (New York: Vintage Books, 1979).

Lynn Caine, *What Did I Do Wrong?: Mothers, Children, Guilt* (New York: Arbor House, 1985).

Helen Colton, *The Gift of Touch* (New York: Seaview/Putnam, 1983)

Norman Cousins, *Anatomy of an Illness* (New York: Bantam Books, 1981).

Patty Duke and Kenneth Duran, *Call Me Anna* (New York: Bantam Books, 1987).

David Elkind, *All Grown Up & No Place to Go* (Reading, PA: Addison-Wesley Publishing Company, 1984).

David Elkind, *The Hurried Child—Growing Up Too Fast Too Soon* (Reading, PA: Addison-Wesley Publishing Company, 1981).

Leonard Felder, Ph.D., *When a Loved One is Ill: How to Take Better Care of Your Loved One, Your Family, and Yourself* (New York: NAL Books, 1990).

Sol Gordon, *When Living Hurts* (New York: Dell Publishing, 1985).

Brent Q. Hafen and Kathryn J. Frandsen, *Youth Suicide: Depression and Loneliness* (Evergreen, CO: Cordillera Press, 1986).

Jo Horne, *Caregiving: Helping an Aging Loved One*

(Prospect, IL: AARP Publications/Scott-Foresman, 1985).

Julie Tallard Johnson, *Hidden Victims* (New York: Doubleday, 1988).

Gerald L. Klerman, Myrna M. Weissman, Bruce J. Rounsaville, and Eve S. Chevron, *Interpersonal Psychotherapy of Depression* (New York: Basic Books, 1984).

Max Lerner, *Wrestling with the Angel: A Memoir of my Triumph Over Illness* (New York: W.W. Norton & Company, 1990).

Rhoda F. Levin, M.S.W., *Heartmates: A Handbook for the Cardiac Spouse* (New York: Pocket Books, 1987).

Francis M. Mondimore, M.D., *Depression: The Mood Disease* (Baltimore: Johns Hopkins University Press, 1990).

Ashley Montagu, *Touching: The Human Significance of the Skin* (New York: Harper & Row, 1971).

Demitri F. Papolos, M.D. and Janice Papolos, *Overcoming Depression* (New York: Harper & Row Publishers, 1988).

Elaine Fantle Shimberg, *Strokes: What Families Should Know* (New York: Ballantine Books, 1990).

Bernie S. Siegel, M.D., *Love, Medicine & Miracles* (New York: Harper & Row, 1986).

Maggie Strong, *Mainstay: For the Well Spouse of the Chronically Ill* (Boston: Little, Brown and Company, 1988).

William Styron, *Darkness Visible: A Memoir of Madness* (New York: Random House, 1990).

Index

Accident-proneness, children and depression, 49
Adolescents and depression
  acting out behaviors, 133
  and communication problems, 139–143
  and eating disorders, 132–134
  risk–taking behaviors, 52–53, 133
Aggression, children and depression, 51
Al-Anon, 209–210
Alcohol
  and drug therapy, 176–177
  over-the-counter tonics, 32
Alcoholism, 13
  and depression, 31–32
  and elderly, 32
  parental, and child's suicide attempts, 194
American Association of Suicidology, 209
American Psychiatric Association
  address, 208
  diagnostic criteria for depression, 39–40
Anorexia, 132
  See also Eating disorders
Antidepressants, types of, 178
Appetite problems, children and depression, 49–50

Beattie, Melody, 159–160
Beck, Dr. Aaron T., 173
Beck Depression Inventory, 173
Benson, Herbert, 108
Biochemical depression. See Endogenous depression
Bipolar depression. See Manic depression
Body language, and communication, 82
Borkovec, Dr. Thomas, 117
Brain damage, stroke, 28–29
Bulemia, 12–13, 132
  physical effects of, 31
  See also Eating disorders

Camp Fire Boys & Girls, 210
Children and depression, 19, 25, 128–152
  accident-proneness, 49
  aggression, 51
  appetite problems, 49–50
  avoiding denial about, 134
  and communication problems, 46
  concentration difficulties, 49
  eating disorders, 49–50, 132–134
  effects on family, 59–60
  energy loss, 50
  environmental factors, 130
  and family meetings, 147–151
  genetic factors, 130
  hyperactivity, 52–53
  incidence of, 129

217

About the Author

Elaine Fantle Shimberg has written numerous books and magazine articles on a variety of medical and family-oriented subjects, and is a member of both the American Medical Writers Association and the American Society of Journalists and Authors. Her book *Relief from IBS: Irritable Bowel Syndrome* was selected as one of the "Best Lay Medical Books for Public Libraries" by the *Library Journal*.

Ms. Shimberg is the mother of five children and lives with her husband Hinks in Tampa, Florida.